BRIDGING A CONTINENT

DISCOVERY AND EXPLORATION

The Reader's Digest Association Limited,
London

BRIDGING A CONTINENT

BY MARTIN HILLMAN

Executive coordinators: Beppie Harrison
John Mason
Design director: Guenther Radtke
Editorial: Elaine Rothman
Picture Editor: Peter Cook
Research: Enid Moore
Sarah Waters
Cartography by Geographical Projects

This edition published in
the United Kingdom and
Republic of Ireland by
The Reader's Digest Association Limited,
25 Berkeley Square, London W1X 6AB,
in association with
Aldus Books Limited, London.

© 1971 Aldus Books Limited, London
Reprinted with amendments 1979
First published in the United Kingdom
1971 by Aldus Books Limited,
17 Conway Street, London W.1
Printed in Great Britain by
Hunt Barnard Web Offset Ltd,
Aylesbury

Contents

Left: early photograph of a wagon train on a narrow mountain trail through the Ute Pass, Colorado.

Frontispiece: wild mustangs still gallop across the Nevada desert.

List of Maps

The illuminated globe shows in blue the
areas that became known as the
explorers of North America walked
and rode through the vast wilderness,
crossing a continent to the Pacific.

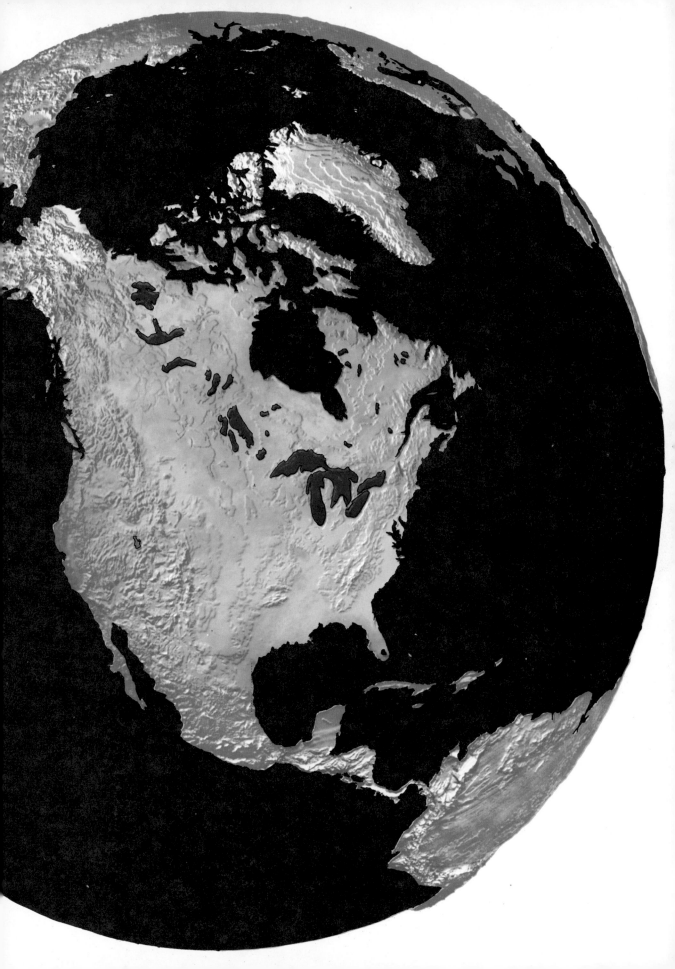

The Spirit of Expansion

1

In 1800, Napoleon Bonaparte, the First Consul of France, worked out a secret treaty with Spain—a treaty that placed over 800,000 square miles of North America's heartland in French hands. That territory, called Louisiana, embraced the vast spread of unexplored wilderness from the northern edge of present-day Texas north to Canada, from the Mississippi west to the Rocky Mountains. It also included the mouth of the Mississippi, and the port of New Orleans. It was about 17 times as large as what we now know as Louisiana.

The treaty seemed to be all to Napoleon's advantage. By trading off a small Italian kingdom for the vast territory of Louisiana, he had re-established France on the North American continent. But, for the man about to take office as American president, Thomas Jefferson, the dealings between France and Spain posed a threat. Louisiana lay next to the western boundary of what was then the United States. Jefferson would much rather have weak Spain as a next-door neighbor than powerful, warlike France. Spain had let the young American republic use New Orleans harbor. Since the great river and its tributaries formed a principal route for outgoing goods, New Orleans was crucial to America's prosperity. But just before giving up control of

Left: in 1800 Louisiana comprised more than 800,000 square miles of virgin territory. Exploration there had been the work not of Americans but of Frenchmen, Spaniards, and British and French Canadians. Much of the land was forested, rimmed with mountains, veined with rivers. Only the Indians traveled it regularly. They lived, as they had always done, by hunting, and at this stage of their relationship with white men were, for the most part, friendly and helpful, willing to trade and to provide guides.

Right: Thomas Jefferson, third President of the United States, was possessed by the great American dream of opening up the West. It was thus appropriate that it was he who was responsible for the purchase of Louisiana from France, which had acquired the territory from Spain.

Louisiana, Spain had closed the port to the United States. That was serious enough. Much worse was having a stronger and ambitious nation such as France in control. For this reason, Jefferson rattled a few threatening sabers and sent an envoy to France to see whether Napoleon could be talked into opening New Orleans again. Jefferson told his envoy to hint that the United States would happily buy the city outright, harbor and all.

Fortunately for the United States, Napoleon's plans for a new French empire in North America ran into trouble. He had just lost nearly 43,000 troops trying to suppress a rebellion of former slaves on the French island of Hispaniola in the West Indies. Those were the troops he had planned to use in the occupation of Louisiana. And in Europe, Napoleon was threatened by war with Britain. The emperor knew that he would soon be too busy in Europe to worry about protecting American colonies, even if he could have sent soldiers and supplies past the British Navy. He also knew that he was going to need money. Jefferson's envoy—James Monroe, himself to be President—was indeed taken aback by an offer from the French to sell not only New

Above: when Napoleon decided to offer Louisiana to the American plenipotentiaries Livingston and Monroe, its boundaries were far from clear. He simply offered the territory as he had acquired it from Spain. When asked to define the bounds of this cession, Napoleon's foreign minister Talleyrand said: "You have a noble bargain, make the most you can of it."

Right: the covered wagon was the classic vehicle by which men, women, and children opened up the American West. There were three wagon trails across the trans-Mississippi West. The first was the Santa Fe trail, and the first American wagons reached Santa Fe in 1822. By 1831 one caravan of a hundred wagons carried over two hundred thousand dollars' worth of goods to the New Mexico capital.

Orleans, but the entire territory of Louisiana.

The United States had soon parted with about $15 million and had received ownership of a tract of land that doubled the size of the American nation. Some countries might have found such an enormous gulp of new territory a little hard to swallow, but not the United States. The Louisiana Purchase seemed to stir in the American people and their leaders an appetite for more. Previously, exploration and colonization of the New World had been left chiefly to the European powers. It had been nearly 200 years since the first British settlers established themselves permanently in Virginia. Now the Americans, some of them having been settled in the New World for six generations, began to realize they had a vast area at their disposal. So the push westward and the expansion of the American frontier began.

The problems which faced these pioneer explorers were many. Just as they were basically unaware of the kind of country they would have to cross, they often lacked the equipment or the skills to do so. The emptiness of the continent was a spur, but the scattered Indian population had influenced the way of life of the settlers. They learned from the Indians how to grow maize, sweet potatoes, and other foods, and how to farm the land. Others took up the rich fur trade and became woodsmen. The settlers were adjusted to the kind of climate and territory they found where they settled and were unprepared for the great differences they would encounter. For example, the Virginians were accustomed to easily navigable rivers, but in the northern parts no network of inland waterways existed. To the west the huge range of the Rocky Mountains and the variation in the climate around them presented new hazards as did the central regions of the recently acquired territory, mistakenly considered the "Great American Desert" for years and years.

Apart from natural difficulties, the farmers knew only the most

Above: North America in 1803, at the time of the Louisiana Purchase. The pink areas were British, gold were Spanish, yellow, Russian, and green, United States.

basic methods of farming, which worked adequately on the virgin fields but tended to exhaust the soil rapidly. And there was an inborn tendency to move on to new pastures before agricultural methods had been improved. In addition the characteristics of the various Indian tribes varied greatly from region to region. Some were helpful and friendly, but others, viewing the white man with dread and suspicion, were hostile and dangerous.

There was friction among fur traders in the Louisiana territory. A border dispute soon arose because no one knew where the borders lay. Spain argued that Louisiana's southern boundary lay on the Red River. The United States claimed it was farther south, on the Rio Grande in Texas. Before a settlement could be reached, American adventurers raided into Spanish territory to trade, and Spanish soldiers charged out from their southwest strongholds to capture and imprison these "trespassers."

Spanish Florida then became the scene of further conflict. A band of American freebooters took over a piece of that area, asked for an-

nexation to the United States, and promptly got it. Eventually the United States were to buy the rest of Florida. But the same treaty which permitted them to do so drew Louisiana's boundary in such a way that Texas remained Spanish. Spain tried appeasement by inviting Americans to colonize portions of Texas. This was inviting the robbers in to share the feast. Soon, however, Mexico fought and won its independence from Spain. The newly independent nation of Mexico included Texas. Within a few years, America's Texans went to war with Mexico and declared their own independence. Later, the United States took up arms against Mexico, and pushed the Spanish-Mexican borders still farther to the southwest.

The main obstacles to United States growth, then, needed no explorers to report on them. To the north and northwest, the British settlements in Canada stood in the way of American advance. To the south and southwest, Mexico sat tight in Texas, and beyond the western mountains in California. The United States had snatched Louisiana from France: Spain had ceded it to France on the condition

Above: the St. Lawrence River was one of the waterways which was used as a highway for expansion by traders and the settlers who followed in their footsteps. The St. Lawrence forms a natural boundary between what have now become the United States and Canada.

Above: the fur trade in North America had been important since the 1600's, but it was to reach its peak by the 1840's, after which it rapidly declined. The bulk of trade was in beaver skins. The trappers went out far beyond the farthest fringes of settlement and civilization to trap and trade furs with the Indians. They returned to the frontier outposts to sell their pelts, often drank and gambled away the proceeds, many returning to the wilds having lost every penny they had gained.

that it would not fall into American hands. But if France had kept Louisiana, the British might have invaded it and taken it over in the war against Napoleon.

Many Americans resented the fact that any part of North America should be British, especially when the biggest piece, Canada, was populated by Loyalists who had deserted the United States during the War of Independence. Other, more practical men also resented the British control of the fur trade and their competition with American fur companies in the forests around the Great Lakes and in the Columbia River Valley.

In the late 1700's, the Canadian fur trade was dominated by two giant companies. The older of the two, the Hudson's Bay Company, founded in London in 1670, controlled the west coast of the great bay, traded with northern Indians, and made few forays into the interior. Its Canadian-based rival, the North West Company, had grown out of a combine of many small enterprises. The Northwesters, as they were called, had found the pickings rich enough to join forces and abandon their often brutal competition.

They collided twice with the Americans when they went southward in force to trap and to trade during the 1780's. Extending all the way to the central Missouri region, they thwarted both Spanish and American fur seekers. They, and some Hudson's Bay men who followed them, ignored the treaty that placed the American border north of the British posts on Lake Superior. They stayed on United States soil well into the 1790's. During this time the Indians of the Ohio country went to war against American settlers all along the frontier, to some extent with British aid and encouragement.

But British help to the Indians did not go far enough. The American General, "Mad Anthony" Wayne—a hero of the Revolution—defeated the tribes at the Battle of Fallen Timbers, in 1794. In the process he laid claim to much new frontier land for the United States. Then, out of British-American efforts to make peace on the border, Jay's Treaty evolved. This treaty was signed in England in November 1794, and was ratified the following June. It finally evicted the British from their Great Lakes posts. But this treaty also allowed Canadian traders full use of waterways south of the border, which gave them new freedom to operate in American territory. Wayne's victory may have ended an Indian war, but it did not lessen the fierce rivalry of the fur traders or put an end to trouble between Britain and the United States.

By the time of Jay's Treaty, both the Americans and the Canadians were struggling for the fur trade in the Pacific Northwest. Alexander

North America. Relief coloring shows the broad central plains and the more rugged coastal and far northern areas.

WHO'S AFRAID?

OR, THE OREGON QUESTION.

Above: "Mad Anthony" Wayne and a small American force defeated the Indian tribes of the old northwest at Fallen Timbers in 1794. He made them sign away their lands to the Americans in a series of treaties, beginning with that of Greenville in 1795. This picture, painted by a member of Wayne's staff, shows American leaders and a group of Indians. Picture by courtesy of the Chicago Historical Society.

Left: the northern boundary of Oregon was the subject of dispute between America and Britain during the 1830's and 1840's. James K. Polk won the presidency in 1844 on the slogan "Fifty-Four Forty or Fight," referring to the American boundary claim. But the British had no wish to fight and the claim was settled amicably in 1846.

Mackenzie, the Canadian explorer and trader, was the first white man to cross the continent and reach the Pacific. A few years later, Meriwether Lewis and William Clark paved the way for Americans. The Northwesters and American companies raced for control of the rich territory in the valley of the Columbia River. That region, soon to be called Old Oregon, was to be hotly contested until the 1840's. When the boundary was drawn at last to end the dispute, the Columbia Valley became American. Until that time, however, Canadian fur traders continued to harass the American frontier.

Slowly, during the first half of the 1800's, the Americans were to take for granted the idea that theirs was to be a transcontinental nation—that it would stretch to the Pacific. They were to see territorial expansion as the American destiny. During these years, too, the first wagon trails westward were to be established. Some Americans even dreamed that Canada and Mexico would also become part of the United States. And, by the 1840's, the idea of expansion had been glorified in the popular slogan "Manifest Destiny." The phrase was invented by John L. O'Sullivan, the editor of a New York City newspaper. In 1845, he wrote, "It is our manifest destiny to overspread

Above: the Alamo, originally the chapel of the San Francisco mission in San Antonio. It was the scene of a famous last stand, when a tiny force of men, including Davy Crockett and Jim Bowie ("the Knife"), fought to the death against a superior Mexican force during the Texan revolution against Mexican rule. The revolution led to Texas becoming a republic and joining the Union in 1845.

17

Right: in 1800, the American West belonged to the Indians who had lived there for thousands of years fishing and hunting buffalo. They had found the best trails across the mountains and rivers and had discovered many mineral deposits. Their methods of travel on water and land were ideally suited to the conditions and they taught the explorers how to live in the open country. But by the end of the century the white men had settled the plains, the buffalo were destroyed, and the Indians had been forced into reservations.

Right: the arid Southwestern territory was entirely different from the broad plains of the prairies across which the early western explorers and settlers moved. This picture shows typical country to the southwest of the Rockies, in Arizona.

the continent allotted by Providence for the free development of our yearly multiplying millions." But even before the politicians picked up the phrase, the spirit of expansion was to push the American frontier toward the Pacific Ocean.

Settlers carried their sense of destiny with them like a banner, as did cattlemen, miners, land speculators, railroad builders, and all the tens of thousands of Americans who pioneered the West. But first of all, it was the explorers who advanced the cause of Manifest Destiny. As soon as Louisiana had been purchased, they began a half-century of learning the hard way about the obstacles to westward growth.

The story of America's half-century of growth and the story of western exploration blend into one. Obviously, explorers and adventurers such as Lewis and Clark, Pike, Frémont, and the rest opened the way for the bearers of Manifest Destiny following in their wake. Traders of all sorts, competing hotly with one another and with foreign interlopers, opened up virgin territory, and in the process helped to claim it for the United States. The United States Army galloped across the West to deal with Indians (who neither knew nor cared who claimed Louisiana) and while doing so opened up the trails and wagon routes to the West. Early pioneers set out on agonized marches to Oregon or Utah or California long before the spread of settlement had even crossed the Mississippi, and often took side trips—sometimes by accident—into unexplored wilderness.

Below: from the Indians with whom they bartered for furs and skins to send back to England, the men of the Hudson's Bay Company learned a great deal. One very important lesson was the technique of fishing through the ice in winter, shown here on the Red River of the North.

Forerunners

2

The Louisiana Purchase may have raised the curtain on the drama of westward exploration, but before the end of the 1700's there had been a prelude of heroic proportions. And it was performed almost entirely by the footloose fur traders of French and British Canada.

America's fur men had stayed content for some time with the lush forests of their old frontier east of the Mississippi, using that river's eastern tributaries as their highways. But traders in Canada had access to the St. Lawrence and Hudson Bay, both of which offered routes deep into the west. The Hudson's Bay Company began an immediate drive in that direction by sending Henry Kelsey inland in 1690 to become the first white man on the Canadian prairies. Sixty-four years later Anthony Henday was sent to penetrate into Blackfoot country within sight of the Rocky Mountains. The Company's French rivals, the Vérendryes, De la Corne, and others, also joined in the competition of exploration. And, following the British takeover of Canada in 1763 as spoils of the Seven Years' War, new rivals filtered out from the east—English-speaking Canadians, most of them backed by Montreal trading firms, and sneeringly called "Pedlars" by the Hudson's Bay Company.

The Pedlars fanned out across the west, plucking furs from Indians who had previously traded with the Hudson's Bay Company, and forcing the older company to take action. The Hudson's Bay Company responded by focusing on the north, where the Pedlars had not yet penetrated. In 1715, they sent William Stewart to the Great Slave Lake region to open up trade with the Chipewyan Indians. He plodded 700 miles across the bleak barrens northwest of Churchill before reaching his destination. Upon his return, he related Indian tales of a great river running past a mountain of pure copper. Because the Pedlars had already seriously reduced the Hudson's Bay Company trade with the Woods Cree and other tribes of the Saskatchewan River Valley, the thought of a northern copper mine seemed rather attractive. For this reason, the Hudson's Bay Company decided to go north again—in the person of Samuel Hearne.

Hearne was a sturdy Londoner, skilled at navigation and surveying, but too new to the fur trade to know about Arctic survival. In 1769, he set out northwest from Churchill with a wholly inadequate supply of food, clothing, and equipment. He was guided by Indians who did not really know their way. As a result, within a month he was back at Churchill, chagrined. But by early 1770, he was ready to make another

Left: Samuel Hearne, whose contact with the Chipewyans was of immense value to the Hudson's Bay Company. Hearne built their first inland post, Cumberland House, on the Saskatchewan River.

Right: a trapper and his wife, with their dog pulling the sledge loaded with partridges. Many trappers married local women and their way of life became a mixture of European and Indian patterns.

trip, with more experienced Indians and more suitable equipment. This time, however, bad weather and broken equipment forced him into long halts along the way before he had halfway reached his objective. Again he turned back.

On the journey back to Churchill, in 1771, he met up with a Chipewyan leader named Matonabbee who knew about the Coppermine River (as it is now known), and he volunteered to take Hearne there. Hearne's knowledge of Arctic survival had improved, so he did not find it necessary to wait for spring to begin the trip. In December of the same year, he set off with Matonabbee and his Chipewyans. He learned a great deal from these Indians. They gathered birchbark along the way for canoe-making so that they could enter navigable waters when necessary. And they also led him to forests where herds of deer wintered, and these supplied the party with food during the cold season.

Their march northward that spring was direct and uneventful. And in July, 1772, they finally reached what Matonabbee informed them was the Coppermine River. But Hearne was terribly disappointed. The river was barely navigable by canoes, and thus useless to the Hudson's Bay Company coastal shipping. The "mountain of copper" did not exist, and, though Hearne found samples of the metal, mining it was not an economic possibility for the mining techniques of the time.

A dejected Hearne began to retrace his steps. He was not even impressed by the fact that when his canoe drifted into the mouth of the Coppermine River, he became the first white man to reach the Arctic Ocean overland. He felt that the journey had been futile, and it seemed only appropriate that on the way home he should lose his watch, his quadrant, and (briefly) his way.

But at least Hearne had improved the Hudson's Bay Company's contacts with the Chipewyans, which were badly needed to offset the Pedlar threat. Because of his experience, the Hudson's Bay Company

Wife returning with a load of Partridges from their Tent. —— By Wm Richards

Left: a Chipewyan warrior. The pioneers of the Hudson's Bay Company and their rivals, the "Pedlars," were very dependent on the local Indians, who acted as their guides.

Above right: a drawing by Samuel Hearne of Lake Athabasca, which illustrates the account of his journey from Prince of Wales Fort around the Hudson Bay region.

Bottom right: the Governor of Red River, Hudson Bay, in a canoe in 1824. The early explorers very quickly adopted the canoe as a convenient means of transportation through the network of rivers which crisscrossed the country.

sent Hearne westward in 1774 to the Saskatchewan River (60 miles above The Pas in present-day Manitoba), to build their first true inland post, Cumberland House, in a key position on the Indians' forest and river routes. The Hudson's Bay Company's trader Matthew Cocking had first located this site during an inland journey to examine the spread of Pedlar influence. But Cumberland House had been constructed too late. For great fur-trade figures, such as the Frobisher brothers, Alexander Henry, James Finlay, and above all Peter Pond, were already pushing deep into the west.

Pond had drifted from the fur forests south of the Great Lakes to join in the rush into the Saskatchewan Valley. He had heard accounts of a very rich fur country farther north. In 1778, he decided to try the trek himself. He took four canoes and a few French-Canadian *voyageurs* (travelers), the superb woodsmen and canoeists who made up the main labor force of the Canadian fur trade. They reached a point some 30 miles south of Lake Athabasca before the rivers froze.

Pond became, then, a major contributor in opening up the northwest's richest fur country. He also tried making maps of the entire Athabasca region, and set up a supply system using *pemmican*, the dried and pounded buffalo meat that was easily transported, and that kept indefinitely.

When the other Pedlars realized that the riches of Athabasca meant plenty of furs for all, they began thinking of transforming their competition into a cooperation. By 1783, the arrangements were made, and the North West Company came into being. But Pond backed off, returning to the United States with his maps of Athabasca and a dream of discovery. As an American, he wanted the new United States Con-

Above: a French Canadian voyageur. The term *voyageur*, meaning a traveler, was used to describe the trappers who hunted in the wilderness. It was also used in New France to describe trappers who operated without a licence. The King of France granted rights to men to engage in the fur trade and these men, in turn, had the right to hire voyageurs to do the actual trapping for them.

Right: a list from the York Factory account book of 1714—1715, which sets out approved trading prices for various commodities. This shows an early attempt that was made to bring some organization to the fur trade.

York Fort America Anno. 1715

The Standard of Trade Viz —
As Settld by the Governour

gress to subsidize him on an expedition that would search for a route from Athabasca over the mountains to the Pacific. But the Canadian northwest must have seemed too far away, then, to interest the young republic; Pond was turned down. He returned to Canada, joined the North West Company, and moved back into Athabasca.

The Northwesters called themselves "Lords of the Lakes and Forests," and usually made good their boast. Every fall, fleets of birchbark canoes, paddled by tireless French voyageurs, fanned out across the whole of the Canadian West. They moved south of Superior to challenge American traders, and near Hudson Bay to challenge the British company. And when the Canadian explorer Alexander Mackenzie had shown the way, they moved out and beyond the Rockies to the Pacific coast.

Meanwhile, in Athabasca, Pond found another famous fur trader, Peter Pangman, who headed a rival company. Pangman sent a group to build a post near Pond's in order to drain off some of the American's trade. One of Pangman's men was killed in a fight with Pond's employees. This alerted the rival traders to the danger of the new rivalry, which could easily have degenerated into a shooting war. As a result, in 1787, the North West Company talked the Pangman group into an amalgamation under the North West Company title. Among the new members was a young Scot who had been Pangman's man in the Churchill area, and who was now sent to complete his fur-trade education with Peter Pond in Athabasca. His name was Alexander Mackenzie,

Above: a painting by Samuel Hearne of Prince of Wales Fort, Manitoba. This was the earliest fort built by the Hudson's Bay Company and became the prototype for those built later. It was surrounded by a stockade (a line of stout posts firmly set into the ground) which protected the buildings from Indian attack.

Left: Sir Alexander Mackenzie (1764?-1820), Scottish-born Canadian explorer. In 1789 he made a remarkable journey from Fort Chipewyan along the Great Slave Lake and down the river—later called the Mackenzie River—to the Arctic. Four years later he crossed the Rocky Mountains from Fort Chipewyan to Cape Menzies, reaching the Pacific coast overland.

Right: an outer trading station at Moose Factory, in the lowlands of Ontario, bordering James Bay. This is a typical inland station and shows fortifications built to protect Hudson's Bay Company men stationed away from company strongholds.

a man in his early twenties who was experienced in the fur trade and fired with restlessness and ambition.

Pond shortly went east to face trial for his alleged involvement with the killing. He was acquitted, but the stain on his name drove him from Canada in 1790. Before he left, though, he had told Mackenzie about the areas of the northwest. Mackenzie soaked up Pond's geographical knowledge, studied his laboriously scrawled maps, and was infected by his obsessive belief in the existence of a route to the Pacific.

In 1789, Mackenzie set off from Fort Chipewyan on Lake Athabasca to lead a group of French Canadians into the north. Fiercely cold weather (though it was June) and ice on the waterways slowed his progress through the Slave Lake region. But in a few weeks, he had crossed the Great Slave Lake itself, leaving it by way of a very wide and terrifyingly swift river. On July 12, he and his men were swept into the tidewaters of the Arctic Ocean. Mackenzie had hoped the river would lead him to the Pacific. As Hearne had done, he retraced

his steps, filled only with disappointment and with no sense of achievement.

After Mackenzie returned to Fort Chipewyan, he felt that he needed better preparation for another attempt. He took some leave and went back to Britain to improve his geographical and navigational education. On the way disappointing news reached him. New navigational measurements which had been compiled at Fort Chipewyan indicated that the Athabasca region was a great deal farther away from the Pacific than Pond or Mackenzie had realized.

In 1792, Mackenzie again left Fort Chipewyan to explore. This time he led a group of six voyageurs, two Indians, and a Scot named Mackay. When they approached the Peace River, they began to travel westward by canoe. After having gone some distance, Mackenzie chose a place for a winter camp to wait until the thaw. While there, he asked the local Indians about the western mountains. His men spent their time building a special birchbark canoe, which was 25 feet long and

Above: the Rockies, a chain of
mountains—in places 400 miles
wide—extending 3,200 miles down
western North America, from northern
Alaska to northern New Mexico.
Several rivers have their source in the
Rocky Mountains, among them the
Columbia, Missouri, Arkansas,
Colorado, and the Rio Grande.

Left: copper kettles and blankets such as these were among the most common articles which the Hudson's Bay Company traded with the Indians.

4 feet 9 inches at the beam. It could carry 3,000 pounds of supplies and equipment and 10 people. Yet, empty, it was light enough to be carried by two men on a *portage* (French for "carriage," which came to mean carrying a boat overland). Mackenzie and his men embarked in this canoe toward the Rocky Mountains in May, 1793.

On paper, Mackenzie's plan seemed simple. He intended to work up to the headwaters of the Peace River in the Rockies, and then seek out a navigable river flowing down the mountains on the westward side. But unexpected difficulties arose. The current of the river was so strong that it taxed every ounce of the voyageurs' strength and canoemanship. The new canoe leaked, causing delays for extra caulking, and the Indians seemed unhappy and likely to desert at any time.

As the days passed, it became harder and harder to make their way up the river. At times the voyageurs had to force the heavy canoe through rocky cascading rapids, or portion out the cargo into enormous packs, staggering on portages through tangled forests and over dangerously steep slopes. It was not long, though, before the mountains were sighted. This encouraged Mackenzie, but he had believed that the Rockies stood like a single wall which sloped down to level ground on the west side. When the expedition clawed its way up to the narrow headwaters of the Peace, they found instead that these mountains were only the most easterly of a series of parallel ranges, with mile after mile of jagged peaks and crags.

Near the Peace River's head, Mackenzie found that it was formed by two streams, known today as the Finlay and the Parsnip. The Finlay seemed to be flowing in the right direction and to be the least torrential. But an Indian had told him that the other stream, though apparently flowing from the south, would later turn in the direction he wanted. Mackenzie took the chance and chose the Parsnip.

Several days of slow progress followed because of the powerful stream currents. Mackenzie had also been warned, by Indian friends, of nearby tribes who might be dangerous. But the first mountain Indians they met were poor Sekani, half-starved and terrified at their first sight of white men. Mackenzie soon won their confidence with food and gifts, and began asking about the river route ahead. One Sekani had heard of a great waterway to the west, which seemed accessible by a short march from the Parsnip's head. Encouraged by this news, the group struggled on up the Parsnip. They were cold and exhausted, but they were not too tired to realize that they had crossed the Great Divide (the highland in North America that separates waters flowing into the Atlantic from those flowing into the Pacific). From that time on any river they traveled would flow westward and they would be traveling with the current.

They soon found their way by a short portage to a narrow waterway that flowed frighteningly fast and was cluttered by trees and rocks. Hidden sandbars added further dangers, and even the voyageurs' skill was not enough to avoid them all. Their canoe finally struck a sandbar, ricocheted onto rocks, and was seriously damaged. Men and cargo were spilled into the torrent. They were luckily washed up into

Above: the type of fast-flowing, tree- and rock-strewn river which the early explorers forced their way along as a matter of routine.
Below: an Indian salmon trap. Such traps take advantage of the fact that salmon swimming upstream can freely enter the first line of nets, but once inside they are unable either to go past the second line of nets and escape upstream, or return the way they have come.

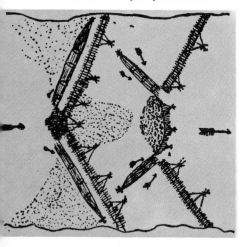

shallow water, and no one was drowned. But most of the stores had been lost, including all of their ammunition.

Every shred of Mackenzie's leadership was needed to raise the morale of his men. He had his group hastily patch the canoe, which was to carry some of the men and part of the remaining stores down the river. The others hacked their way about two miles a day through the tangle of mountain bush. By June 17, they had forced their way to the banks of the great river mentioned by the Sekani.

In better spirits, the company swept down the new river and found it was tributary to a still greater waterway known now as the Fraser. Mackenzie had no idea what lay ahead of him in the mountain canyons of that river. But he was more concerned just then with the local Indians. He had seen houses, salmon traps, and other signs of Indian habitation. He soon found that one tribe, called Carriers, were as warlike as they were civilized. A party of these Indians fled before the white men, and two Indian translators whom Mackenzie sent after the Carriers were fired upon.

Two days later Mackenzie's party met Indians of another tribe who threatened the group with death if they landed. Mackenzie promptly landed—by himself—and his courage so impressed the Indians that they approached and listened to what he had to say. He soon won them over and delighted them with gifts of trinkets. They conducted him to their camp, and told him fearful tales of the Fraser River's impassable

Above: a Plains Indian *parflêche* (an envelope made from dried rawhide) used to store pemmican. Pemmican was made of diced lean meat, dried in the sun, pounded, and mixed into a paste with melted fat. Sometimes flavored with berries, pemmican would keep indefinitely in these containers.

rapids and the perpendicular rock walls of its canyons. They also told him of fierce Indians along those canyons who killed strangers first and inquired about them afterward. But Mackenzie suspected exaggeration, and was stubbornly determined to go on.

When he returned to the river, he met another band of Indians, who were more friendly but just as full of dire warnings about the river. Mackenzie considered continuing overland, and returned up river until July 4.

By now the treacheries of the Fraser were apparent, so the group took to the land and cached the canoe and a supply of pemmican on the riverside. They plodded for 10 days in the face of grueling scrambles up the steep sides of the Coast Ranges, while their food supply and their energy were rapidly diminishing. They stumbled through a hailstorm and through drifting snow in a mountain pass; they slid down into a valley and found it clogged with forest. But their luck finally changed when they met up with some Bella Coola Indians, who fed them with salmon and told them in sign language that the Dean River flowing past their village led to salt water. Mackenzie had come far closer to the sea than he had dared to dream.

The Indians provided Mackenzie and his men with two canoes, and the party returned to the river once more. A day later they reached over the sides of their canoes to find that the water was salty. They were in a narrow fiord-like inlet (North Bentinck Arm). Gulls flew overhead, and the men saw porpoises and seals in the water. Mackenzie was torn between his desire to reach the open sea and the pressing need to begin the return trip as quickly as possible. For food supplies were running low, and it was a long way back to Fort Chipewyan.

Mackenzie was also nervous about some Bella Bella Indians camped in the inlet whom he believed to have been ill-treated by some seafaring fur traders. He had heard that, as a result, they were hostile toward the white man. This soon proved to be true, for the Indians began to harass Mackenzie's men, steal from their camp, and threaten an all-out attack. At one point, while Mackenzie was on land alone, several of them rushed him with daggers. But they stopped and backed away when he coolly raised his gun.

Although Mackenzie kept the threatened Indian attack from materializing, it was clear that he had to leave the inlet for home. So the group returned upstream to the friendly Bella Coolas, and then marched back over their former path to their cached canoe. In better spirits now, and with their food stores replenished, the men rapidly forced their way up the Fraser and its tributary. Not even their extreme weariness, the numbing cold of the water, or an unexplained injury to Mackenzie's ankle could hold them up.

On August 16, they crossed the Great Divide, and soon portaged

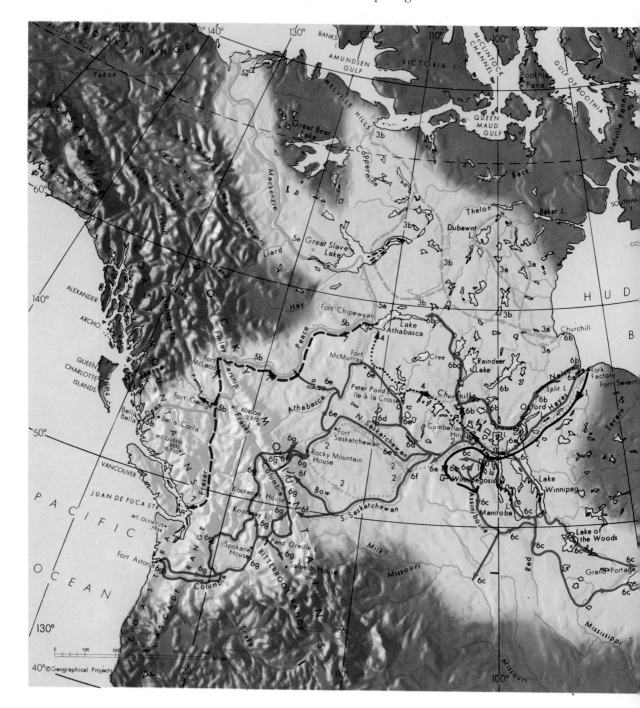

their way to the Peace River. The weather was warm, great buffalo herds grazed beside the river banks, and the current swirled their canoe at high speed toward Lake Athabasca. In one day they had covered a distance that had taken them seven days to travel going the other way.

On August 24, in a flurry of flag-waving and rifle fire, Mackenzie's group swept up to Fort Chipewyan. Fifteen hundred miles behind them lay the evidence of the first overland crossing of the continent, a rock bearing the following inscription: "Alex. Mackenzie from Canada by land 22d July 1793."

Left: Canada, with the vast northwest highlighted in green, showing the routes of the men who explored there in the years between 1650 and 1811.

Kelsey	1	1690
Henday	2	1755
Hearne	3a	1770
	3b	1771-2
Pond	4	1778
Mackenzie	5a	1789
	5b	1792-3
Thompson	6a	1790
	6b	1792-7
	6c	1797-8
	6d	1798
	6e	1799
	6f	1800-2
	6g	1807-11
Fraser	7	1808

Above: Mackenzie's Rock, commemorating the first overland crossing of the continent. The rock bears the inscription: "Alex. Mackenzie from Canada by land 22d July 1793."

Corps of Discovery

3

President Thomas Jefferson may have been startled when France offered the whole of the Louisiana Territory for sale in 1803, but he was far from unprepared. In 1793, he had been instrumental in sending a French scientist westward into Kentucky, although nothing concrete had developed from that journey. Then, a few months before his envoy went to Paris to discuss Louisiana, Jefferson had quietly directed his private secretary to undertake certain studies. These included geography, navigation, and other subjects that would be needed on an exploring trip to the Pacific.

Jefferson's private secretary was a man named Meriwether Lewis, a 29-year-old Virginian, frontiersman, and soldier. He had served in the army in Ohio with a former Army lieutenant and friend, William Clark. They had enormous respect for each other as soldiers and woodsmen, and were now going to work together again as partners for Jefferson. The two were to share joint command of the expedition, though, in fact, Lewis became the overall leader.

News of the Louisiana Purchase speeded up their preparations. Lewis had copies of most of the available maps of the northwest, which included those of Captain Vancouver and Alexander Mackenzie. He had abundant supplies and equipment ready, among which was a collapsible canoe he had invented himself (but which turned out to be impracticable). Boatbuilders were adapting—to Lewis' designs—a 55-foot keelboat, which could be sailed, rowed, poled like a raft, or, as a last resort, towed from the riverbank. The boat carried two wooden canoe-like rowing boats called pirogues. In addition, it was to hold instruments, weapons and ammunition, tools, provisions, spare clothing, 21 bales of goods for trading with Indians, and more than 40 men.

Lewis recruited some of his men in Pittsburgh, and took them down the Ohio River in August, 1803, to join Clark. The trip was interrupted by the usual obstacles of river travel such as shallows, fogs, and squalls. But in late October they reached Louisville, where they picked up Clark and his Negro slave, York.

Clark had done some recruiting, too. A group of tough young Kentuckians had signed on, of whom the brothers Reuben and Joseph Field were the most outstanding frontiersmen. But the expedition's most valuable acquisition was George Drouillard, half French and half Shawnee, an expert with a rifle, as well as being a scout, a tracker, and a woodsman. He made even the Field brothers seem like novices. Aside from a few French-Canadian rivermen who were to run

Below: (right) Meriwether Lewis (1774—1809) and (left) William Clark (1770—1838), leaders of the first United States overland expedition to the Pacific. From May, 1804 to September, 1806, the expedition covered over 4,000 miles, meeting Indian tribes never previously seen by white men, and keeping a valuable record of scientific observations. Despite the hardships and exposure they suffered, only one man died on the expedition. Lewis was made governor of northern Louisiana in 1807. Clark was made superintendent of Indian affairs at St. Louis in 1807 and territorial governor of Missouri in 1813.

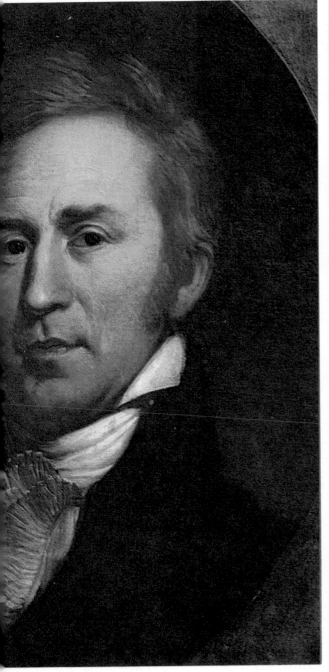

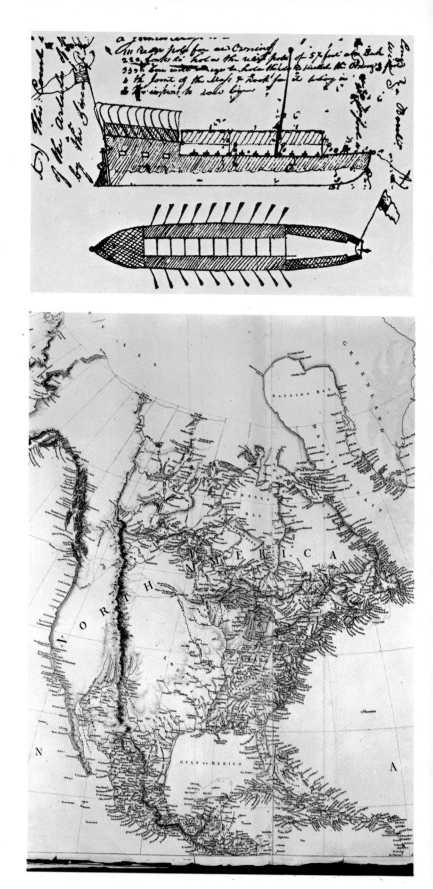

Above right: sketch from the "Field Notes" of Lieutenant William Clark, showing the expedition's Missouri River keelboat. A keelboat is a long, shallow craft, pointed at both ends, which is either sailed, rowed, poled, or towed from the riverbank.

Below right: a map of America by Aaron Arrowsmith dated 1804. This would have been the type of map taken on the expedition and shows how little information was available at the time. The western part of the continent is almost completely blank, with only a theoretical range of mountains sketched in to the west of the Mississippi River.

the boat, the remainder of the expedition's strength was made up of regular soldiers.

Jefferson had made it clear to Lewis that his job would be to explore the upper Missouri region for a water route linking with the Columbia River; to make maps and charts of the river and its valleys; to contact the Indians of the region; and to examine the soil and the animal and plant life. In other words, the exploration was to be of a scientific nature.

In late 1803, Lewis and Clark took their men and their boat up the Mississippi to St. Louis, where they spent the winter. Waiting for spring and for the formal transfer of Louisiana to the United States, Lewis remained in St. Louis to attend to diplomatic business while Clark took the party up the river to St. Charles. Clark wrote the following description of St. Charles: "This village is about one mile in length, situated on the North Side of the Missourie at the foot of a hill from which it takes its name *Peetiete Coete* or the *Little hill*. This Village Contns about 100 houses, the most of them small and indefferent and about 450

Below: a lithograph by Felix Achille St. Aulaire showing a keelboat under sail on the Mississippi in 1832.

inhabitents Chiefly French, those people appear Pore, polite & harmonious."

On May 21, 1804, after Lewis had joined the party, the keelboat left St. Charles. As Clark wrote in the journal: "All the forepart of the Day arranging our party and procureing the different articles necessary for them at this place. Set out at half passed three oClock under three Cheers from the gentlemen on the bank and proceeded on to the head of the Island (which is Situated on the Stbd. Side) 3 miles. Soon after we Set out to day a hard Wind from the W. S. W. accompanied with a hard rain, which lasted with Short intervales all night."

Clark managed to push the boat on the average 15 miles a day, while Lewis wandered the shore making scientific observations. In late

Below: Sioux Indians moving camp. The Indians of the Sioux tribe became well-known for their courage and fighting ability and were particularly feared by the early explorers because of their ferocity.

May, they reached La Charrette, the most westerly fragment of civilization on the river. Beyond that tiny settlement lay the unknown wilderness.

By July, they were deep into wild Indian country, but had not met up with any Indians. Then, during a halt at the junction with the Platte River, Drouillard came in from hunting accompanied by a Missouri Indian. A few days later a large company of Oto and Missouri came to visit. Lewis spoke to the assemblage about the United States control of Louisiana and the need for peace between Indians and Americans. And he was delighted and encouraged by the Indians' cordial acceptance of these sentiments. But Lewis also knew that the unpredictable Sioux were out there, too, and might not receive him so cordially. He made an attempt to invite the Sioux for a gathering: "We set the Praries on fire as a signal for the Soues to Come to the River," but there was no response. Drouillard, though, encountered some Omaha Indians, and through them Lewis made contact with the Sioux nation. On August 31 (at Council Bluffs), he opened his first council with the most feared Indians in the Missouri country.

Lewis saw little of the legendary ferocity of the Sioux in this first contact, and the expedition parted from the Indians on the best of terms. But Lewis kept his perspective. He had originally planned to send his soldiers back to St. Louis in the pirogues in the autumn, but now he decided to keep them where they were for the winter, in case of Indian

Above: watercolor by Alfred Jacob Miller of 1837 of a Sioux Indian, which captures the pride and confidence of an Indian brave. The Indians' attitude toward white men veered between hostility and curiosity, depending largely on the white men they (or their tribe, or nearby tribes) had encountered before.

hostilities. Besides, extra hands were needed to prepare their winter camp.

For a while, the Corps spent some idyllic days, hunting the abundant autumn game, while Lewis was happily engrossed with natural history. He wrote about his observations in great detail: "Having for many days past confined myself to the boat, I determined to devote this day to amuse myself on shore with my gun and view the interior of the country lying between the river and the Corvus Creek.... One quarter of a mile in rear of our camp which was situated in a fine open grove of cotton wood passed a grove of plumb trees loaded with fruit and now ripe, observed but little difference betwen this fruit and that of similar kind common to the Atlantic States... a great number of wolves of the small kind, halks [hawks] and some pole-cats were to be seen... to the West a high range of hills, strech across the country from N. to S. and appeared distant about 20 miles; they are not very extensive as I could plainly observe their rise and termination no rock appeared on them and the sides were covered with virdue similar to that of the plains this senery already rich pleasing and beatiful was still farther hightened by immence herds of Buffaloe, deer, Elk, and Antelopes which we saw in every direction feeding on the hills and plains."

But the mood was shattered by the keelboat's approach to another Sioux camp, which turned out to be far from peaceable. When Lewis tried to begin a council, the chiefs reacted with suspicion and belligerence. He made an attempt to change their attitudes by inviting them to the keelboat for gifts of whiskey, but to no avail. Clark escorted the chiefs back to shore in a pirogue, and at that point the warriors menacingly surrounded the boat. Clark could not return, they said, until further gifts were made and more respects were paid to the Sioux leaders. No one knows whether the Indians were just testing the white man's mettle or actually planning violence. But Lewis and Clark handled the moment perfectly with calm and counter-threat. Clark, alone on the beach, drew his sword and stood firm. On the keelboat, Lewis ordered his riflemen to the ready, but withheld the order to fire. And the Sioux, with spears and arrows against rifles, backed down and released the pirogue. Clark related this incident in the journal as follows: "Met in Council at 12 oClock and after Smokeing, Cap. Lewis proceeded to Deliver a Speech which we (were) oblige(d) to Curtail for want of a good interpreter ....

"Envited those Cheifs on board to Show them our boat and such

Above: an Azimuth compass of about 1770, a surveyor's compass of the type available to Lewis and Clark. Below: a pocket sextant made in the late 1700's. Using a compass, a sextant, and a watch, the explorers were able to make rough maps, chart rivers, and fix their positions.

Left: an illustration showing
Captain Clark and his men building
a line of huts, from "a journal of
the voyages and travels of a corps
of discovery, under the Command of
Captain Lewis and Captain Clark of
the Army of the United States, from
the mouth of the River Missouri
through the Interior parts of North
America to the Pacific Ocean during
the years 1804, 1805, and 1806,"
by Patrick Gass, published in 1807.

Above: a Shoshoni woman catching a horse. The women of the Shoshoni tribe proved themselves to be very self-sufficient. Sacagawea, the young Shoshoni wife of a French trader who joined the expedition as an interpreter, was a great help to Lewis and Clark along the trail.

Curiossities as was Strange to them, we gave them ¼ a glass of whiskey which they appeared to be verry fond of, Sucked the bottle after it was out & Soon began to be troublesom, one the 2d Cheif assumeing Drunkness, as a Cloake for his rascally intentions I went with those Cheifs *(in one of the Perogues with 5 men—3 & 2 Inds.)* (which left the boat with great reluctiance) to Shore with a view of reconsileing those men to us, as Soon as I landed the Perogue three of their young Men Seased the Cable of the Perogue, *(in which we had pressents &c)* the Cheifs Soldr. Huged the mast, and the 2d Chief was verry insolent both in words & justures *(pretended Drunkenness & Staggered up against me)* declareing I should not go on, Stateing he had not receved presents sufficent from us, his justures were of Such a personal nature I felt My self Compeled to Draw my Sward *(and Made a Signal to the boat to prepare for action)* at this Motion Capt. Lewis ordered all under arms in the boat, those with me also Showed a Disposition to Defend themselves and me, the grand Chief then took hold of the roap & ordered the young Warrers away, I felt My Self warm & Spoke in verry positive terms.

"Most of the Warriers appeared to have ther Bows strung and took out their arrows from the quiver. as I *(being surrounded)* was not permited to return, I Sent all the men except 2 Inps. [Interpreters] to the boat, the perogue Soon returned with about 12 of our determined men ready for any event. this movement caused a no: of the Indians to withdraw at a distance, Their treatment to me was verry rough & I think justified roughness on my part, they all lift [left] my Perogue, and Councild with themselves the result I could not lern and nearly all went off after remaining in this Situation Some time I offered my hand to the 1. & 2. Chiefs who refusd. to receve it. I turned off & went with my men on board the perogue, I had not prosd. more the [than] 10 paces before the 1st Cheif 3rd & 2nd Brave Men Waded in after me. I took them in & went on board.

"We proceeded on about 1 Mile & anchored out off a Willow Island placed a guard on Shore to protect the Cooks & a guard in the boat, fastened the Perogue to the boat, I call this Island bad humered Island as we were in a bad Humer."

For a while the Sioux seemed pacified, even friendly. But a flurry of trouble arose again when Lewis finally decided to set sail. For the Sioux had been piratically terrorizing river traders and they did not want a powerful force of white men so deep within their country. But again the explorers' combination of coolness and firepower kept

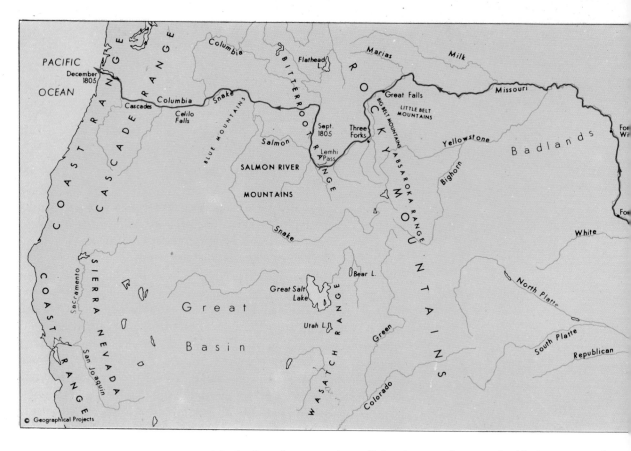

the Indians from starting a fight. As a result, peace had been preserved, and the Corps of Discovery sailed on.

Because the weather had turned cold, windy, and wet, a winter campsite was urgently needed. One was found on Mandan country by the time of the first snow, and its construction was begun in November. A stout log cantonment called Fort Mandan was soon put up, and the Corps settled in for the tedious winter wait.

There were some minor diversions during those winter months such as hunting parties, Christmas festivities, and the like. Lewis made contact occasionally with North West Company fur traders, among them being Antoine Larocque, probably the first white man to explore into the Yellowstone River Valley. Of more importance, though, was a freelance French trader who joined the Corps. He brought with him two Indian wives. One of them, a Shoshoni girl (Sacagawea), was later to prove to be of help to the expedition.

When spring freed the keelboat from river ice, Lewis sent it back east with some of the soldiers. The narrowing river demanded smaller craft, and so the Corps, with Mandan help, made six dugout canoes to supplement the two pirogues. On April 7, 1805, Lewis and Clark and about 30 men moved out again northwestward.

"So far," Lewis wrote in a letter at this time, "we have experienced more difficulty from the navigation of the Missouri than danger from the savages...." And those difficulties worsened as they passed into Dakota badlands, where even fur traders had not traveled. But by late

46

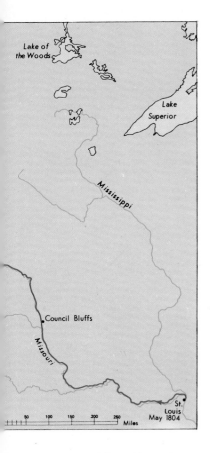

Above: the route followed by the Lewis and Clark expedition westward from St. Louis across the Great Divide to the coast of the Pacific.

April they had reached the junction with the Yellowstone River, which was located in rugged foothill country. This region held some animals which were strange to them: mountain sheep, mules, deer, and grizzly bears. The Corps had heard terrifying tales of the ferocious bears; they soon found them to be no exaggeration. When Clark and Drouillard were hunting, they encountered a grizzly that pursued them back to the river even though the hunters had shot the bear several times before it died. Later, another grizzly chased six hunters out of the forest and into the river in spite of eight bullet wounds.

While bears were keeping the hunters busy, the Missouri was occupying the rivermen. On a number of occasions, squalls nearly upset the canoes. The strengthening current forced the men to give up rowing and turn to towing. And, in June, the Corps reached a fork in the river, for which they had been entirely unprepared. They had no idea which branch to take. Clark decided to explore a short distance up the northern branch while Lewis took the other. Their men felt that the northern branch (which Lewis called Maria's River, now the Marias) was more navigable than the other. Understandably, they clamored that it was the true Missouri. Lewis was convinced otherwise. But the expedition's esprit de corps showed itself when the men followed Lewis without a murmur even though they disagreed with him. Lewis was very soon proved right, though, for the boats came within earshot of the Great Falls, which they knew were a feature of the true Missouri. In Lewis' words: "I retired to the shade of a tree where I determined to fix my

Right: an American explorer up a tree to escape a bear. Clark originally reported that the stories of the ferociousness of the grizzly bear were exaggerated. However, on further acquaintance he found the tales were true and that the grizzly would attack without provocation.

Above: a scene, showing a typical camp in the moonlight, which became part of the legend of the West. For almost a hundred years from the time of Lewis and Clark, such scenes were enacted nightly in the wilderness.

camp for the present and dispatch a man in the morning to inform Capt. C. and the party of my success in finding the falls and settle in their minds all further doubts as to the Missouri."

They began a grueling portage around the 90-foot cascade. Lewis, roaming the countryside as usual, almost idly shot a buffalo for camp meat—and very idly neglected to reload. In nearly cost him his life, for out of nowhere came a grizzly bear at full charge. Lewis ran for the river while trying to reload, but the bear was gaining on him too rapidly. His only weapon was his *espontoon* (a short pike widely used at that time). At the water's edge, Lewis clutched it and turned to face the onrush of the grizzly. For no good reason the bear stopped short, and then wheeled and galloped off into the bush. And Lewis, puzzled but hardly shaken, reloaded his gun and wandered peacefully back to the camp at the Falls.

There he found his men making a crude wagon to carry the boats on the portage. They had to repair the wagon constantly, because deep mud and rough ground weakened its structure. But finally, in mid-July, the back-breaking, 18-mile detour was over, and the Corps went back on the river to force their way up into the Rocky Mountains.

The expedition now found itself in the country of the Shoshoni (or Snake) Indians, the people of Sacagawea, the wife of the French trader. But though there were plenty of signs of Indians, they still had not met up with mountain Indians from whom they needed advice about travel through the Rockies. Lewis and Clark had been shocked, as Mackenzie was, to find that the Rockies were not a single wall of mountains. They still believed that the Columbia headwaters would be waiting for them, after a short overland trek across the Continental or Great Divide.

By late July, they had reached another expected landmark, the Missouri's Three Forks. They camped there for some time in order to rest the men who were worn out from towing the boats against the shallow but violent mountain stream. As was written in the journal: "The men were so much fortiegued today that they wished much that navigation was at an end that they might go by land." But they continued on the southwest branch of the river (Lewis called it the Jefferson). Lewis, with Drouillard and others, left the party, to forge ahead on land and look for the Shoshoni. They roamed the river valley for days while Clark and the others dragged the boats up the now unnavigable stream. Soon the Jefferson itself forked, and Lewis thought that the boats would never be able to pass that point. He also realized that the Corps had climbed high up into the mountains, and had come near to the source of the Missouri and the Great Divide: "the mountains do not appear very high in any direction tho' the tops of some of them are partially covered with snow. this convinces me that we have ascended to a great hight since we have entered the rocky Mountains, yet the ascent had been so gradual along the vallies that it was scarcely perceptable by land." In fact, two more days of climbing and wandering brought Lewis through what is now known as Lemhi Pass. He found a rivulet on the other side, and was ecstatically convinced that it fed directly into the Columbia. Unfortunately, the river was not navigable. Now the need for Indian help grew even more desperate. The day after crossing the Divide, Lewis met a band of Shoshoni.

Drouillard was sent to bring back Clark and the rest of the company with all possible speed. After they arrived, the Corps were able to obtain anything they wanted from the tribe, but at a dear price. Lewis, Clark and their fellow travellers replenished their supplies of food, and were also able to acquire much needed horses, some Shoshoni guides,

Above: this picture of the San Juan mountains, Colorado, shows the gradual slopes by which they can be climbed. The explorers were surprised at the heights they attained without being aware that they had been climbing.

Right: a mural by E. S. Paxon shows Sacagawea pointing out the country of her childhood to Lewis and Clark at Three Forks, western Montana.

and information about westward routes. Because of the oncoming August frosts and autumn snows, the expedition hastily left the Shoshoni to continue their journey.

They cached their canoes and some equipment on the Jefferson River, and then struggled off on heavily laden horses over underbrush-choked mountain trails looking for navigable water. But in late August, they decided to turn north to the Bitterroot Valley in order to strike an Indian trail described by the Shoshoni. The trail was rocky and precipitous; horses crippled themselves and some even fell down the slopes. The hunting grew poor and the men grew hungry. Once or twice the men killed and ate one of the more useless horses; the rest of the time they ate leftover bits of bear grease, scraps of maize, or nothing. They were now 6,000 to 7,000 feet up, and on September 16, they suffered the first heavy snowfall of the mountain winter, which caught them on a rugged and treacherous ridge: "began to Snow about 3 hours before Day and continued all day the Snow in the morning 4 inches deep . . . at 12 oClock we halted on the top of the mountain to worm and dry our Selves a little as well as to let our horses rest and graze a little on Some long grass which I observed, I have been wet and as cold in every part as I ever was in my life, indeed I was at one time fearfull

my feet would freeze in the thin Mockirsons which I wore."

They soon found before them lower, less rugged terrain, and a creek which they were sure would lead to the Columbia River. A headlong descent by the starving, weakened men brought them to a hospitable Nez Percé camp, where the Indians fed them on dried salmon. Here the weather was warmer and game more plentiful.

After they had been fed and had rested, the Corps began to travel again. Within a few days they had reached the Clearwater River, a tributary of the Snake which led to the Columbia. On October 7, they

Right: a typical peril of river travel is shown in this illustration from Patrick Gass's Journal of 1807. The canoe has struck a tree and over-turned, spilling the occupants out into the swirling water of the river.

Above: a sketch map by Clark showing the mouth of the Columbia River, from the original journals of the Lewis and Clark expedition 1804—1806.

embarked in their canoes on the river. They battled through the rapids without pause and stopped only briefly to buy fish and dog meat from riverside Indians.

From the Clearwater they paddled into the Snake River, which had even more rapids. But Lewis refused to hesitate. He even ordered his men to run the risk of rocks and cascades rather than make a portage. Several times canoes overturned and sank, but always, miraculously, the men in them survived. They managed to salvage the canoes, repair them, and keep going.

On October 16, almost without warning, the canoemen found themselves on the broad waters of the Columbia, rushing toward the sea: "after getting Safely over the rapid and haveing taken Diner Set out and proceeded on Seven miles to the junction of this river and the Columbia which joins from the N.W. In every direction from the junction of those rivers the country is one continued plain low and rises from the water gradually, except a range of high Countrey on the opposit Side about 2 miles distant from the Collumbia." They were continually held up because of the rapids and dangerous stretches of water which ran through the Cascade Range. And yet Lewis and Clark urged their men on because of the approaching winter.

When they reached the Narrows of the Columbia, Lewis saw the water "boiling and whorling in every direction" over jagged rocks, but the impatient Corps flung their canoes through the obstacles, without any damaging effects. A longer portage then had to be made around the ferocious waters of the Cascades. Needless to say, the men resented the waste of another few days. By early November, though, the Cascades were behind them; they had overcome the last mountain obstacle and were moving through tidewater.

Within a few days, the river widened into a broad bay. The Corps thought (mistakenly) that they could see the Pacific. "Ocian in view! O, the joy!" wrote Clark in his journal, but that joy turned to misery when rough water and torrential rain drove them to camp under the bay's sheer cliffs. They huddled there for days, with their soaked buckskin shirts rotting on their backs, until quieter weather allowed them to embark again. Within a short time, they had paddled into the Columbia's estuary, with the open sea almost anticlimactically spread before them.

Later, while a spot for a winter camp was being chosen, Clark carved on a pine tree a message that consciously echoed Alexander Mackenzie:

Above: one of the great successes of
the Lewis and Clark expedition was
the friendly relationship it maintained with the majority of the
Indian tribes it encountered. Clark
particularly had a special gift for
dealing with the Indians and he
remained an "ambassador" to and for
Indians long after the expedition.

Right: "The Captive Charger" by the
American artist Charles F. Wimar,
records one of the many hazards that
Lewis and Clark, like other explorers,
had to face—the fact that the
Indians were immensely interested
(often in an acquisitive way) in their
belongings, especially their horses.

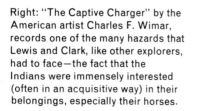

"William Clark, December 3rd, 1805. By land from the U. States in 1804 and 1805."

Wintering on the coast brought rain, boredom, and swarms of curious Chinook Indians. Needless to say, the men were all delighted to start out on the return trip. Before leaving for home, though, the party distributed some lists of their names to the Indians in the area. The object of such lists was stated as follows: "The object of this list is, that through the medium of some civilized person who may see the same, it may be made known to the informed world, that the party

Above: lithograph published by Julius Hutawa in St. Louis, Missouri, showing St. Louis in the mid-1800's. The small pictures around the edge show the principal buildings of the city at that time. Lying between the Appalachian Mountains and the Rockies. St. Louis is on the main course of the Mississippi. In 1806, when Lewis and Clark finally returned to St. Louis, it was a great fur-trading center. Picture by courtesy of the Chicago Historical Society.

consisting of the persons whose names are hereunto annexed, and who were sent out by the government of the U'States in May 1804 to explore the interior of the Continent of North America, did penetrate the same by way of the Missouri and Columbia Rivers, to the discharge of the latter into the Pacific Ocean, where they arrived on the 14th November 1805, and from whence they departed the [blank in MS] day of March, 1806 on their return to the United States by the same route they had come out."

On March 23, they began their fight upstream against the Columbia's swollen torrent, hugging the bank and portaging often. But in spite of all caution, their canoes suffered constant damage. And when they found the roaring narrows wholly impassable by water, they abandoned canoe travel and transferred their baggage to horses, which they acquired from the Indians.

Throughout April, they marched overland, painfully but steadily, toward the Clearwater River and the Bitterroot Valley beyond it. During the winter, Lewis and Clark had rightly decided that their original route, through Lemhi Pass, had taken them too far southward. Therefore, they intended to head straight across the mountains (overland) from the Bitterroot and, hopefully, to come to the Missouri in the vicinity of the Great Falls.

Friendly Nez Percé and Walla Walla Indians kept them supplied with food, a few extra horses, and information about adequate mountain trails. The march progressed with little drama, except for constant and careful negotiations for food and other assistance at various Indian villages. In late June, they reached the Bitterroot Valley and stopped to take stock.

They decided to divide the party and carry out some necessary explorations. Lewis, Drouillard, the Field brothers, and a few others were to set out on a likely route across the Divide, head straight for the Missouri, and then descend to the Great Falls. Lewis would leave a few men there, and turn north with the rest to explore the Marias River, the north branch of which had puzzled them before. Clark was to set out with his party south through the mountains to the Jefferson River. He would then send some men by water to the Great Falls and take the others overland to explore along the Yellowstone River.

Clark's party moved off on July 3, on a usable trail, and crossed the Continental Divide through Gibbons Pass to reach the Missouri's Three Forks. A sergeant took some men downriver to the Falls, while

Above: a medicine man of the Blackfoot tribe. Medicine men knew a little simple medicine; they could set broken bones and understood the value of herbs. But most of their "medicine" was based on the Indian belief that illness was brought about by evil spirits and the medicine man's cures involved charms, incantations, magic rituals, and elaborate ceremonies. He would wear the mask of the particular spirit involved so that he could speak with the spirit directly himself.

Clark (whose group included Sacagawea) traveled easily overland to the Yellowstone River. Their exploration proved uneventful, except when some Crow Indians stole half of their horses. But the group managed comfortably to reach the Missouri again in early August.

Lewis and his party chose a suitable easterly trail that brought them over the Divide by a pass now called Lewis and Clark Pass. The Sun River then carried them down to the Missouri. Toward late July, Lewis, Drouillard, and the Field boys set off up the Marias River, wondering whether it would bring them as far north as the Saskatchewan Valley. They were also wary because they had now entered the hunting ground of the notorious Blackfoot Indians.

Before the end of July, their fears proved justified, for they met up with a band of eight Piegans (one of the three main tribes of the Blackfoot Confederacy). The Piegans seemed cool but not hostile. Lewis rashly invited them to camp with his party and to hold council. During the night, however, the Blackfoot tried to steal the whites' rifles. A scuffle broke out as the explorers awoke. Reuben Field saw one Blackfoot running off with two of the rifles. Both Field boys were famous for their running and Reuben easily overtook the Indian. They fought, and Reuben killed the Blackfoot with his knife. The other Indians had raced out of the camp to drive off the whites' horses. Lewis and Drouillard ran after them, and a fight developed. Lewis shot an Indian, retreated to the camp, and quickly gathered his men. They were soon galloping at high speed for the Missouri. With only brief rests, the expedition traveled over 100 miles in the next 24 hours. There they met up with the soldiers awaiting them, and set off downriver, on July 28, to meet Clark near the mouth of the Yellowstone. They moved at top speed, for they knew a large force of Blackfoot would be scouring the region for them.

Lewis and the main body of the Corps met Clark's party in mid-August, and within a few days they re-entered Mandan country (what is now North Dakota). The return was eased by the mountain shortcuts, and they traveled 1,900 miles in less than five months.

On September 20, 1806, they paddled into La Charrette. Three days later, more than two years after the start of their 5,000-mile journey, the Lewis and Clark expedition made a triumphant entry into St. Louis: "we rose early took the Cheif to the public store & furnished him with Some clothes &c. took an early breckfast with Colo. Hunt

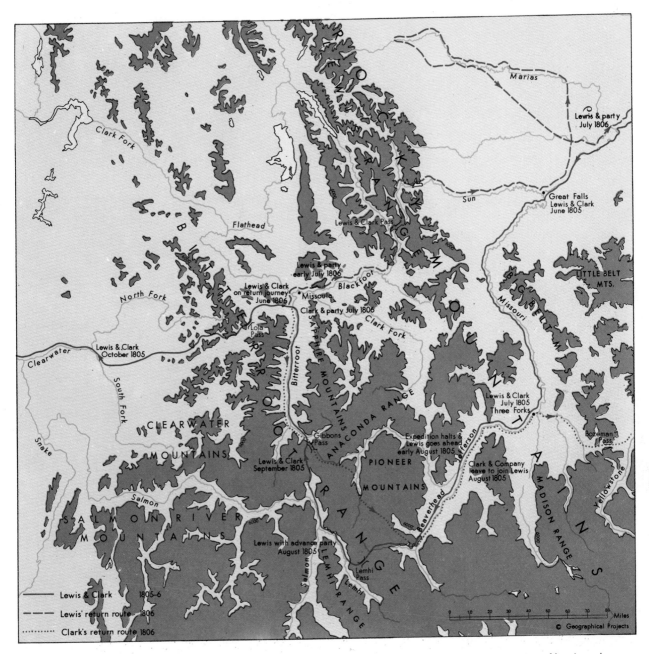

Detail from the journey of Lewis and Clark, showing the separate routes taken by the groups on their return east through the mountains. The green shows the lower-lying ground, the brown the mountains themselves.

and Set out decended to the Mississippi and down that river to St. Louis at which place we arived about 12 oClock. we Suffered the party to fire off their pieces as a Salute to the Town. we were met by all the village and received a harty welcom from it's inhabitants &c."

Lewis and Clark had not found a wholly manageable, all-water route to the Pacific (i.e. a Northwest Passage), or anything remotely re-resembling one. Like Alexander Mackenzie, they felt disappointed. But they *had* found a northwest region vastly larger and richer than anyone had visualized. Now, thanks to them, the United States knew a great deal more about those invaluable lands, and proceeded to lay claim to them. In the next four decades, swarms of explorers, traders, and settlers were to spend their efforts consolidating that claim.

Edging Toward the Southwest

4

While Lewis and Clark were battling with the Missouri River in northwest Louisiana Territory, an expedition to blaze a trail into the southwest was being planned. It was to be led by a young army lieutenant named Zebulon M. Pike. The idea for the expedition arose out of a political situation contrived by two ambitious men.

When Louisiana had been formally purchased, an army general named James Wilkinson had been appointed its first governor, and commander of the western army. The general was an ambitious schemer and opportunist, as was Aaron Burr, a politician who had helped Wilkinson become governor. Burr may have had dreams of power that involved getting Spain and America into war, during which he hoped to peel off a piece of Spanish America as his own independent nation. Wilkinson found these plans parallel to his own, and knew that he was in an excellent position to implement them. He was the governor, and he was also in the pay of the Spanish—to inform them about any United States' threat to the southwest.

In order to further his ambitions of a possible takeover of the whole of Louisiana, Wilkinson decided to have the territory investigated

Left: deserted cliff dwellings common in the southwest, originally inhabited by Indians who proved particularly vulnerable to the white men.

Right: James Wilkinson (1757–1825), American soldier and adventurer. He became governor of the part of Louisiana north of the 33rd parallel in 1805. In his joint roles of army commander and governor, he attempted to fulfill his ambition to conquer Spain's Mexican provinces and to set up his own independent nation.

Above: Zebulon Pike (1779–1813), American explorer and soldier. He led the expedition which explored the upper Mississippi region in 1805. Then in 1806 he headed an expedition to the headwaters of the Arkansas and Red rivers. Pike was military agent in New Orleans in 1809–1810 and Brigadier-General in 1813. He saw active service in the War of 1812 and was killed by a falling rock as his victorious soldiers were breaking into a British garrison at York (now Toronto), Canada, in 1813.

in greater depth before exploring the southwest. For this reason, he first sent Pike north to find the source of the Mississippi and to locate likely sites for United States Army posts in the region. He was also to report on British fur trading there. In August, 1805, Pike began his trip up the Mississippi from a settlement near St. Louis. Pike wrote in his journal: "On the 9th day of August, 1805, the exploring party, consisting of Lieutenant Pike, one sergeant, two corporals and seventeen privates, left their encampment near St. Louis in a keelboat, seventy feet long, provisioned for four months; in order to make a survey of the river Mississippi to its source."

At that time Lewis and Clark were in Shoshoni country, struggling across the Rocky Mountains. By comparison, Pike's journey was uneventful. His meeting with Indians along the way proved satisfactory; even the Sioux treated him with courtesy.

Rain and fog brought discomfort and reminded them that winter was approaching. Therefore, in mid-October, Pike set his men to work on a winter camp near what is now Little Falls, Minnesota. By the time the camp was finished and provisioned, the river had begun to freeze. Pike had sleds made and in early December he and some of the men set off on foot along the river. Mishaps were frequent, but more or less trivial. The main problem was that sleds toppled into stretches of open water, or broke down. The journals of Pike's expedition reported the difficulties: "Whilst proceeding up the river, the foremost of the sleds, which contained all the ammunition, and the baggage of Mr. Pike, fell through the ice. The men had to get into the river, up to their middles in water, to recover the articles; and on an examination of them it was found that all their cartridges, and several pounds of battle powder [gun powder] was spoilt, what they happened to have in kegs was saved, or they must have given up... the voyage for want of the means of supplying themselves with provisions."

When the expedition had reached a fork in the upper Mississippi, Pike chose the branch now called Leech Lake River as being the true course to the source of the Mississippi. But he was proved wrong. For this branch led him to Leech Lake, when, in fact, the other branch led farther north to Lake Itasca, the river's true source. Of course, Pike was tracing a frozen river in mid-winter, with numerous small rivulets and obscure channels from which to choose. At that time, apparently only one white man, a trader named Morrison, had been to Lake Itasca, and he was not aware that it had any connection with the Mississippi.

Right: much of Pike's exploration was undertaken during the winter months in conditions such as these. Difficulties due to the unfamiliar terrain were made even more hazardous by the bitter mountain conditions and inadequate food supplies.

None of the Northwesters living in the area had been able to fix the source either. Therefore, Lake Itasca was left in obscurity until 1832 when H. R. Schoolcraft was finally to proclaim it as the Mississippi's origin and give it its current name.

Pike retraced his steps along the river, and on April 30th, 1806, the expedition floated into St. Louis. The journal account says: "At daylight on the morning of the 30th of April they reached the portage de Sioux, where Capt. Mancy's men were landed, and directed to march across the land to the cantonment. Mr. Pike walked through the village, which has not more than about twenty houses, built of squared logs. They arrived at Saint Louis about noon, after an absence of eight months and twenty two days," By then, Governor Wilkinson's plans for the southwest were beginning to come to a head.

The Spanish holdings in what is now the United States included Arizona, New Mexico, most of California and Texas, and parts of Utah, Colorado, Nevada, and Oklahoma. But then there were no fixed bound-

Above: Mandan Indians crossing the frozen Missouri. The Indian method of travel on frozen rivers was one of the skills that the white men were forced to learn. Although they did not travel in winter from choice, circumstances often made it necessary.

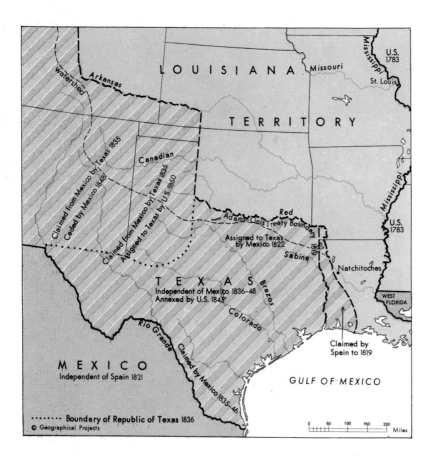

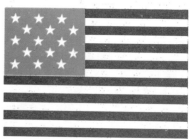

Above: the American flag of 1795, with
fifteen stripes and fifteen stars,
and the Spanish colonial flag of the
same period. The flags represent
the powers facing each other in the
southwest during Pike's explorations.

Above: the southwest of what is now
the United States, and Mexico,
showing the disputed area between
the Red and Rio Grande rivers, where
Pike was exploring in the years
1806-1807.

aries, so that the enormous central and southern region where the South
Platte, Arkansas, and Red rivers flowed became violently disputed
territory. By the time Pike returned from the north, frontier tensions in this region had almost reached a state of war. Much of the conflict had been created by the explorers who had been sent to this
controversial territory by the President. For instance, in October, 1804,
Jefferson sponsored two scientists, William Dunbar and George
Hunter, on a voyage up the Red River. But hostile Indians had diverted
them to the Ouachita River (Ozark plateau), and in the end they covered
little ground and brought back information of secondary value. In 1806,
Jefferson tried again, sending an army captain named Sparks and a surveyor named Thomas Freeman with 19 men up the Red River. They
covered 600 miles before being turned back by the Spanish cavalry.

Wilkinson was now ready to explore the southwest of Louisiana.

He authorized Pike to form and lead this expedition. Pike was to look for the headwaters of the Red River, by way of the Arkansas. But his trip was to begin by escorting some Osage Indians to their home (on the Missouri-Kansas border) and to mediate in an Osage-Kansas Indian war. Pike was ordered to enter Spanish territory, but on no account was he to do anything that might give offense to the Spanish authorities. He was ordered to look at as much of the Spanish territory in the southwest as he could.

Wilkinson informed the Spanish authorities that Pike was on his way into their territory. Undoubtedly he knew that Spanish soldiers would rush out to capture Pike. In this way, Pike would be certain to reach Santa Fe, though as a prisoner, and would then be able to do some close-range spying. Or his capture might create an international incident that would further the Wilkinson-Burr plans—or both. It seems

Above: Pawnee Indians migrating. The Indian tribes were moved about by both the Spanish and Americans whenever it suited the governments' convenience. Indian wars and Spanish/American rivalries were both occasions for voluntary or involuntary movement of the Indians.

Above: Pikes Peak, Colorado, found by Zebulon Pike in 1806, in the Rampart range of the Rocky Mountains. Below: Mexican soldiers, typical of those that Pike would have seen.

quite probable that Pike was completely unaware of this intrigue.

Pike set out from the Mississippi on July 15, 1806, heading for Osage country in the company of 21 men, including Governor Wilkinson's son James, also an army lieutenant: "....We sailed from the landing at Bele Fontaine about 3 o'clock P.M., in two boats. Our party consisted of two lieutenants, one surgeon, one sergeant, two corporals, 16 privates and one interpreter. We had also under our charge chiefs of the Osage and Pawnees, who, with a number of women and children, had been to Washington. These Indians had been redeemed from captivity among the Potawatomies, and were now to be returned to their friends at the Osage towns."

They rowed and poled two barges up the Osage River and duly delivered their 51 charges. After addressing the Indians on the subject of United States displeasure with Indian wars, Pike acquired horses and set off *north*west toward the Republican River. This brief detour was made in order to contact the Pawnee and to inform them of America's ownership of their territory.

The Pawnee proved none too friendly because some weeks earlier a large detachment of Spanish cavalry had visited the region (probably looking for Pike), poisoning the Pawnee minds against American interlopers. When Pike informed the Pawnee that they now owed allegiance to the Stars and Stripes and not to Spain, the Indians grew uncooperative and menacing. They threatened to stop Pike by force from traveling west: "Wednesday, October 1st. Paid a visit to town and had a very long conversation with the Chief, who urged everything in his power to induce us to turn back. Finally, he very candidly told us that the Spaniards wished to have gone further into our country, but he induced them to give up the idea; that they had listened to him and he wished us to do the same; that he had promised the Spaniards to act as he now did, and that we must proceed no further, or he must stop us by force of arms. My reply was that I had been sent out by our great father to explore the western country, to visit all his red children, to make peace between them, and turn them from shedding blood; ...I had not seen any blood in our path; but he must know that the young warriors of his great American father were not women, to be turned back by words; that I should therefore proceed, and if he thought proper to stop me, he could attempt it; but we were men, well armed and would sell our lives at a dear rate to his nation; that we knew our great father would send his young warriors there to gather our bones and revenge our deaths on his people when our spirits would rejoice in hearing our exploits sung in the war-songs of our Chiefs." In spite of this grand oration, Pike was disturbed by the Chief's threats of force. But Pike did as he said he would and rode off toward the Arkansas River. He impudently followed the broad swathe of a trail that the Spanish cavalry had made on their way back to Santa Fe.

By October 18, Pike reached the Arkansas. Lieutenant Wilkinson then returned with some men to the Mississippi with reports. Pike took the remaining men and pushed westward up the Arkansas, toward the mountains—and the Spanish possessions. The headwaters of the Red River, his ostensible goal, lay almost due south.

Wilkinson's party traveled in coracle-like canoes, which had to be dragged over miles of shallows on the lower Arkansas, and which he finally abandoned when an autumn frost brought ice to the river. With his clothing in tatters and his ammunition running short, the young lieutenant grimly refused to stop and build shelters for the winter. Instead he forced his way along the unpredictable waterway to the Mississippi, and on to New Orleans. At the Arkansas' other extreme Pike had been meeting as much difficulty with equal determination.

Pike's group rode on horseback along the bank of the river. The valley deepened into a gorge, and the trail grew rougher; their

Above: the sort of clothes worn by most western trappers and explorers. Although made of buckskin, the material used by the Indians, the style shows strong European influence. The skins held in the body warmth, and protected the wearer from wind.

tired horses began to give out fast. Then, on November 15, the men saw what looked like a small blue cloud to the west. A spyglass revealed it as a thrusting mountain peak, and the men cheered aloud at having come in sight of the Rocky Mountains: "At two o'clock in the afternoon I thought I could distinguish a mountain to our right, which appeared like a small blue cloud; view it with the spy glass, and was still more confirmed in my conjecture, yet only communicated it to Dr. Robinson, who was in front with me; but in half an hour they appeared in full view before us. When our small party arrived on the hill they with one accord gave three cheers to the Mexican mountains [the main chain of the Rocky Mountains]. Their appearance can easily be imagined by those who have crossed the Alleghenies; but their sides were whiter, as if covered with snow, or a white stone."

By November 25, they were camped at the vast peak's base, or so they thought, until they set out to climb it. They found that they had climbed a spur, and that the "Grand Peak" lay a day's march away. Pike asserted that it would never be climbed by man, for he judged its height at over 18,000 feet above sea level.

This side trip to the mountain, which later became Pikes Peak, was beset by the fierce Colorado winter. As freeze-up settled in, the march became agony. The horses grew weaker because of the lack of grass. The men were numb with cold and had frostbitten feet. Still following what he thought was the Spanish trail, Pike struck northward, cross-country, and on December 13 came to a frozen river, which he correctly identified as the Platte (i.e. the South Platte). The expedition struggled south again, but when they found themselves back at the Arkansas River, Pike concluded that it was the Red: "After pointing out the ground for the encampment, the doctor and myself went on to make discoveries, as was our usual custom, and in about four miles' march we struck what we supposed to be Red River... which here was about 25 yards wide, ran with great rapidity, and was full of rocks. We returned to the party with the news, which gave general pleasure. Determined to remain a day or two in order to examine the source."

But the men were in no condition for clear thinking. They were freezing in their cotton rags and had been sleeping on snow and frozen ground. Many were without blankets because they had cut them up to wrap their feet in. Horses were collapsing under them at a rapid rate. In these circumstances, geographical inaccuracy can be forgiven. At least the buffalo remained plentiful, so that they did not starve.

Above: the kind of environment in which Pike and his party found themselves during the winter of 1806, in the mountains of Colorado. The rugged, snow-covered mountain passes, with no grass for the horses to eat, and little or no shelter for the men, did not stop them, however, and most of the party survived the ordeal.

Within a short time, though, Pike realized his mistake about the Arkansas. He decided, therefore, to build a winter camp, deposit some of the supplies and two men there, and go on foot to find the Red River.

During the grueling march, two of the men developed such badly frozen feet that Pike, reluctantly, had to leave them behind. He left ample provisions and promised to send help as soon as he could. Snow, weariness, and 70-pound packs slowed his progress, but despair changed into elation when he came to a creek (the Medano), and found near it a large river flowing southeast. Pike jubilantly announced that they had found the Red. In fact, they had circumvented the source of the Red and they were now on the Rio Grande's northern headwaters.

The party built a stockade there and settled in for the winter, with

the exception of Dr. Robinson. The doctor had been commissioned
to find the fur trader Baptiste Lelande in Santa Fe, to get some money
that Lelande owed his backer in Kaskaskia.

Shortly after Dr. Robinson set out, some Spanish soldiers rode up
to announce that he had been picked up by outriders, and that Pike
was trespassing on Spanish territory. The Spanish commanding officer
addressed Pike as follows: "Sir, the governor of New Mexico being
informed you had missed your route, ordered me to offer you, in his
name, mules, horses, money, or whatever you might stand in need of
to conduct you to the head of Red River; as from Santa Fe to where it

Left: Spaniards escorting Pike into Santa Fe after his arrest for trespassing onto Spanish territory. From Santa Fe, Pike and the men arrested with him were taken to Chihuahua and then by a roundabout route to the American frontier.

is sometimes navigable is eight days' journey, and we have guides and the routes of the traders to conduct us."

"What," said I interrupting him, "is not this the Red River?"

"No sir! The Rio de Norte."

"I immediately ordered my flag to be taken down and rolled up, feeling how... I had committed myself in entering their territory, and conscious that they must have positive orders to take me in."

"He now added that he had provided 100 mules and horses to take in my party and baggage, and how anxious his Excellency was to see me at Santa Fe." In March, 1807, Pike was escorted into Santa Fe

Below: a typical settler's room in New Mexico in the 1800's. Such rooms were sparsely furnished, the dim light contrasting severely with the brilliant sunlight outdoors. Despite the intense heat outside, the room was very cool due to the thickness of the exterior adobe walls.

Below: Aaron Burr (1756—1836) the politician who joined with Wilkinson in a bid to conquer Mexico. When the scheme failed, Wilkinson betrayed Burr and he was tried for treason in 1807. Though officially cleared, public opinion was against him and he fled to Europe for five years.

by the Spanish. He was treated with courtesy, but his notes and papers were confiscated and he was clearly in custody.

At that point, Pike's journey of exploration ended. The Santa Fe authorities sent him to Mexico, and from there he was escorted through Texas back to the frontier settlement of Natchitoches. He returned home on July 1, 1807, to find himself in the center of a political storm.

During Pike's journey (in 1806), border tensions had deepened in the delicate area between the Sabine and Red rivers. Governor Wilkinson was ordered to lead the western army to Natchitoches; he reached the frontier in September, ready to profit by the coming war. But he was thwarted. The Spanish did not arrest Pike that year, no international incident sparked off hostilities, and the government had begun to probe into the doings of Aaron Burr and his associates.

Wilkinson, therefore, cut his losses. He betrayed Burr to Jefferson, revealing the whole plot—except for his own role. Then he negotiated with the Spanish, setting up a neutral zone west of Natchitoches that would prevent quarreling until a boundary treaty could be agreed upon. In June, 1807, Burr was charged with treason. And though the charges did not stick (he was acquitted in late 1807), his reputation

was greatly harmed. Wilkinson, too, was affected and became the object of an investigation. He was officially cleared, twice, but was replaced in October, 1806, as governor of Louisiana by John Graham.

Pike's denial of any knowledge of the conspiracy seems to have been generally accepted, and he remained something of a popular figure. But the shadow of Burr and Wilkinson, to some extent, prevented his achievement being as widely hailed as that of Lewis and Clark. And yet history shows that Pike's exploration proved just as valuable to United States expansion. His detailed descriptions of the Kansas-Colorado area, New Mexico, and Texas opened the way for other explorers and traders.

At the same time, Pike's journey had one invidious, long-range effect. He had called the Arkansas River region "sterile." In the published account of his findings he described the *entire* central plains region as "incapable of cultivation" and likely to become "as celebrated as the sandy deserts of Africa." Pike, therefore, made the first authoritative statement of an idea that was to hold currency for years: the idea of the "Great American Desert." Others after him echoed this phrase, thereby focusing attention on the more obvious riches of the Far West.

Above: the painting of Stone City, Iowa, by Grant Wood, suggests the immense fertility of the area, and completely refutes Pike's idea that the central plains were not worth cultivating. One of the reasons why settlement jumped from the east coast to the west coast was because of the great myth that the prairies were an uncultivable desert.

73

Right: this page from Lewis and Clark's journal, in which they described what they saw and drew illustrative maps, shows the sort of detailed information that the early expeditions produced on various parts of the Great West.

Fur Traders and Mountain Men
5

Above: the North West Company's fur trader Simon Fraser. Between 1805 and 1807 he traveled across the Rockies from eastern Canada setting up trading posts and contributing much to Canada's overland fur-trade route. In 1808, Fraser explored the river which now bears his name.

The northwest Rocky Mountains take in an enormous area—the states of Oregon, Washington, Idaho, parts of Wyoming and Montana, and Canada's British Columbia. Alexander Mackenzie and Lewis and Clark brought back information in abundance about this region. But the picture as a whole was still very sketchy. People were still guessing about the geography of the area. Some of the guesses proved rather far-fetched, like Clark's idea that the Yellowstone River would lead neatly south to Santa Fe.

It was necessary, therefore, for other explorers to venture into the

Below: a "Universal Instrument," surveying equipment available in the early 1800's. Such instruments were used to measure the horizontal angle between two far objects, or angles of elevation or depression.

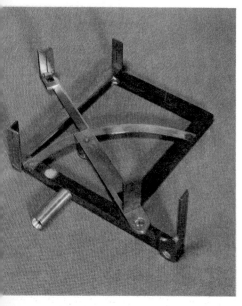

high country to fill out the geographical picture. And they came, all of them, not as government-backed expeditions, but as fur traders who were looking for beaver. The Canadians concentrated first on the area Mackenzie had passed through, and then they gradually moved south. The Americans went to the upper Missouri first, and gradually moved west. Both groups collided briefly on the Pacific coast and later shifted their main operations southeast, down around the head-waters of the Snake River.

Simon Fraser first led the traders of the North West Company into what is now British Columbia. From 1805-1807, he roamed the northern Rockies, building forts and trading. In 1808 he set out to follow the turbulent river that Mackenzie had thought was the upper Columbia.

The river seemed to be nothing but mile upon mile of rocky narrows and rapids, cascades, and whirlpools, which occurred in unbroken, exhausting succession. Fraser's voyageurs labored heroically to keep the expedition's four canoes afloat, but the strain proved too great. When the precipitous canyons allowed, Fraser took his men off the

river. They marched alongside it, through fiercely tangled forest, and walked along rock-strewn trails where only mountain goats and Indians knew of secure footholds. Finally, after hundreds of miles and near starvation, they reached the navigable stretch of the river. They took to canoes again and headed down river toward the Pacific.

Even then Fraser did not reach the open sea. Hostile Indians turned him back in the Strait of Georgia. But before retracing those painful steps, Fraser checked his instruments and found that according to Mackenzie's calculations he should be at 46° latitude. Instead he was far north of that latitude on which he knew the Columbia lay. He had proved Mackenzie wrong, and found another river, now the Fraser.

At about the same time, David Thompson, a brilliant surveyor as well as a fur trader, had crossed the mountains to look elsewhere for a Northwester route to the coast. Thompson traveled many south-bound waterways, including the Kootenay River down into Idaho, and had soon formed a clear picture of British Columbia's southern rivers. He had also located the headwaters of the Columbia.

Above: a painting by Paul Kane in 1847 of the falls at Colville on the Columbia River. Rising in the ice fields of the Rockies, the Columbia is the largest river that flows into the Pacific Ocean from the North American continent.

But Indian troubles and fur trading kept him from embarking on that river until 1811. He then fought his way down the river, with three voyageurs and five Indians in an oversized canoe. They traveled through the narrows and cascades that Lewis and Clark had conquered. When Thompson reached the Pacific in July, he had shown that the Northwesters could travel by water across the continent from the St. Lawrence to the Columbia.

The Northwesters in British Columbia were the first fur men to carry the trade west of the mountains. In America, their counterparts concentrated on the upper Missouri. A shrewd St. Louis businessman, Manuel Lisa, had seen the potential of the high country even before Lewis and Clark had finished their expedition. In April, 1807, Lisa led 42 men, with George Drouillard as guide, up the Missouri. They overcame all the obstacles of that river, including the truculent Sioux and Arikara Indians. By late October, they had erected a fort on the Yellowstone River, near its junction with the Bighorn. Lisa then sent his men out into the wilds to trap and to trade.

Among those men was John Colter, who had trapped that region widely after leaving Lewis and Clark, and who had met Lisa's party on their way upriver. But the Yellowstone Valley held no further interest for him. So he left Lisa's fort to begin a looping route that would take him over approximately 500 miles of rugged mountain country, where no white man had been before. And Colter went alone, in the dead of winter, carrying only a handgun and a 30-pound pack on his back.

He roamed the Bighorn, and then explored up the Yellowstone. There he stumbled on the pits of bubbling mud in what is now Yellowstone National Park. Colters Hell it was called, but few people believed his story. He also crossed the Great Divide in the towering Grand Teton Mountains, becoming the first white man to look down into

Above: "Escape from Blackfeet" by Alfred Jacob Miller, about 1837. The Blackfoot, a group of Plains tribes living between the Mississippi River and the Rocky Mountains, were the strongest and most aggressive tribe on the northwestern plains, as many of the early explorers (particularly John Colter) came to realize.

Left: Grand Teton mountains, part of Grand Teton National Park, established to preserve an area of unusual scenic beauty in northwestern Wyoming. John Colter, an American trapper turned mountain man, was the first white man to explore the region and the reports of his exploits have formed the basis of information about America's frontier expansion in that area.

Jackson's Hole. It was an amazing achievement, which was made all the more heroic by his brushes with hostile Indians, struggles on improvised snowshoes against mountain blizzards, and long periods of hunger when game was scarce.

After his solo journey south along the Bighorn, Colter trapped around the upper Missouri, and at one point fell in with a group of Flathead Indians. He was with them when a superior force of Blackfoot ambushed the group. Colter was hit in the leg, but managed to pour such a withering fire into the Blackfoot ranks that he turned the battle against them. He made his way back to Lisa's fort, recuperated, and returned to the wilderness.

Upon his return, he was immediately captured by the vengeful Blackfoot. By way of a slow death, they disarmed him, stripped him naked, and let him run, with the whole Blackfoot band screeching after him. Colter ran, pushing himself to the limit. He outdistanced all his pursuers but one. Turning suddenly, Colter grabbed the Indian's spear and killed him instantly. Running again, he reached the Madison River, plunged into the freezing water, and hid under a cluster of driftwood.

Above: German-born John Jacob Astor, who emigrated to New York in 1784. Picture by courtesy of the Chicago Historical Society.

Above: moccasins of deerskin or mooseskin, with elaborate beadwork embroidery. These are typical examples of Indian footwear which the mountain men quickly adopted.

Meanwhile, the furious Indians scoured the riverbanks for him. After some hours, Colter emerged from the driftwood, clambered up a sheer cliff, and began walking on gashed and bleeding feet to Lisa's fort about 200 miles away. In spite of underbrush, thorns, rocky terrain, swarms of insects, freezing nights, and barely any food, in less than 11 days he reached the fort. Soon after, Colter left the fur trade for the comparative peace of a Missouri frontier farm.

By 1810, a great many mountain men were roaming the Rockies of Idaho. They were the leftovers from Lisa's group or newcomers connected with a new venture that took the United States fur trade to the coast. The venture was owned by a New York merchant named John Jacob Astor. He sent a group of men by ship—the *Tonquin*—around the Horn of South America to build Fort Astoria at the mouth of the Columbia. While the ship was en route, another Astor employee, named Wilson Price Hunt, led a party of 62 men westward out of St. Louis for the same destination.

Their journey was sheer disaster. Recruiting difficulties delayed them, and ice on the Missouri forced them to stop for the winter after only a few hundred miles. Fear of the Blackfoot then kept them off the river, so they started, with only enough horses for carrying baggage, across South Dakota and Wyoming to the Bighorn Mountains. They reached Wind River (a branch of the Bighorn) in the fall of 1811.

Game grew more scarce as they passed from the Wind to the Green River and over the mountain ranges to the Snake. Finding that stream unnavigable, they continued on foot. The group decided to split, scattering in smaller groups to find food and a passable route. Some men dropped out, hoping to survive on their own. The others went on, at times eating their own moccasins, wandering lost in the deepening canyon of the Snake, and trying, in vain, to run canoes down that ferocious torrent.

In spite of a winter's torment in the mountains, most of the party reached Astoria by early 1812. They found the place in a sorry state. The *Tonquin* had been blown up during an Indian attack farther up the coast, and during the previous summer, David Thompson had floated down the Columbia to announce that Canada, i.e. the North West Company, claimed that river's territory. Astor had to be informed, so in June, 1812, young Robert Stuart set off with a group of men to retrace Hunt's overland path.

Stuart was out in the wilds when the War of 1812 broke out. He knew

nothing of the arrival at Astoria (in early 1813) of a Northwester force demanding the fort's surrender and threatening the Astorians with the imminent arrival of a British warship. In fact, the warship did not arrive until November of that year, by which time the Astorians had saved face and cut their losses by selling the fort to the North West Company.

As a result, Stuart's ordeal turned out to be pointless. But it resulted in a discovery that would revolutionize all travel to and through the western mountains. For when they reached the Bear River, Stuart's group drifted southeast where they came upon a broad vista of low, rolling hills with mountains looming on either side. They had found South Pass, which was no narrow corridor but a 20-mile-wide gap in the eastern mountain range, which led out to some of the great central rivers. This discovery proved to America that the Columbia was accessible by means other than laborious boat-and-portage river travel. Wagons would now be able to roll all the way to the coast through this low-elevation doorway through the mountains.

But wagons were not yet ready to roll, and the fur traders had not yet finished with the region. With the Canadians firmly in charge of the Columbia Valley, the American emphasis shifted back to the mountains. And even there they met strong competition from the North West Company, especially after the region had come under the leadership (in 1816) of a dynamic, 300-pound Scot named Donald McKenzie.

McKenzie had been an Astorian with Hunt's party and knew the region well. As a Northwester, he fanned his men out through the Columbia Valley, and then led a thrust into the rich beaver country of Idaho (roughly between the headwaters of the Snake, Wind, Green, and Bear rivers). McKenzie himself thoroughly explored the Snake River country, firmly locating that river's navigable parts and some

Above: Fort Astoria in 1813, the central depot set up by John Jacob Astor in 1811 at the mouth of the Columbia River. It was seized by the English two years later.

Below: Northwester Donald McKenzie, who organized the Canadian company's fur-gathering operations in the West. Instead of fixed posts, he introduced mobile trapping brigades.

Above: the aptly-named Snake River
has its source in Wyoming, just to
the south of Yellowstone Park. It
leaves Wyoming and flows sinuously
westward through Idaho, turning
northward at the Oregon border to
form a natural boundary between the
two states. Flowing westward again,
it joins the Columbia River near
Pasco, Washington, 1,038 miles from
its source. This was the area that
McKenzie explored so thoroughly. No
longer known for beaver hunting, it
is now predominantly a farming area.

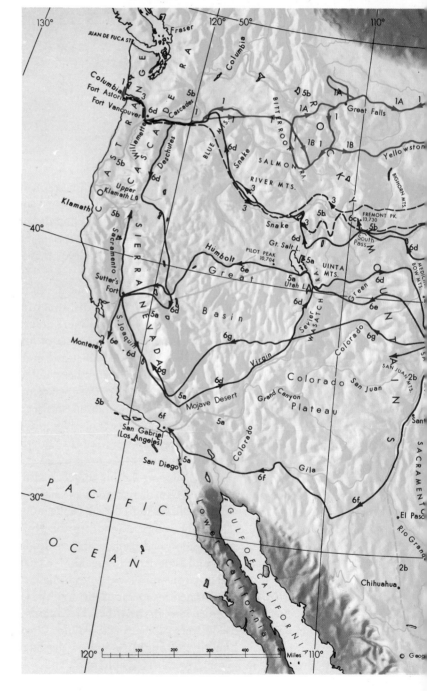

Right: The United States, and the routes
of the most important explorers from
Lewis and Clark to Frémont. The green
highlights the area of exploration.

shortcuts (such as the Boise River). Meanwhile, other Northwesters ranged all over the region of the Snake and Green rivers, penetrating as far south as Bear Lake, the most southerly exploration in the mountains up to that time. Against such rivals, the slow-moving, conservative Hudson's Bay Company lost every battle in the wilderness. The rivalry between the companies continued for several years, during which time they opened up Canada as far as the Pacific.

McKenzie retired in 1831, ten years after the North West Company amalgamated with the Hudson's Bay Company under the latter's ban-

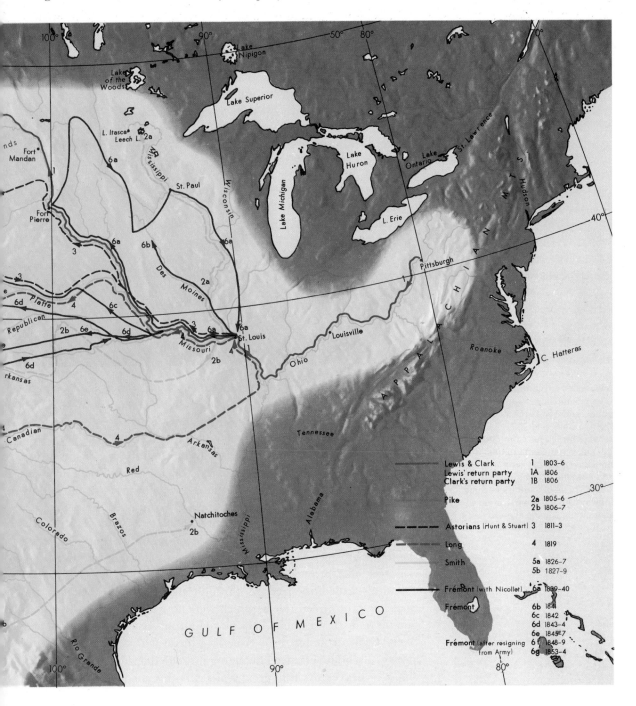

Lewis & Clark	1	1803–6
Lewis' return party	1A	1806
Clark's return party	1B	1806
Pike	2a	1805–6
	2b	1806–7
Astorians (Hunt & Stuart)	3	1811–3
Long	4	1819
Smith	5a	1826–7
	5b	1827–9
Frémont (with Nicollet)	6a	1839–40
Frémont	6b	1841
	6c	1842
	6d	1843–4
	6e	1845–7
Frémont (after resigning from Army)	6f	1848–9
	6g	1853–4

ner. His successors found that American competition was stepping up. In 1824, the Northwester Alexander Ross, operating north in the Clearwater River region, met a group of American mountain men led by a youth named Jedediah Smith. Ross did not know it, but this young man represented the most dangerous competition of all.

Smith, only 25 years old at that time, was to become as legendary a mountain man and explorer as John Colter. He had come west as part of a major fur-trading assault, which was organized by William Henry Ashley out of St. Louis. In 1823, the Ashley men went west in two

Above: early in the 1820's the fur trade became more highly organized. Annual rendezvous (gatherings of trappers) were established, at which furs were traded for ammunition, food, and other commodities. Such a rendezvous took place on the Green River, near the Wyoming/Utah border, in 1824. These gatherings became an important annual event, not only for trading, but as a social event and a time for exchanging news.

parties, one headed for the Yellowstone and the other, led by Smith, through the heart of the Black Hills into Bighorn country. With Smith went other mountain men, only slightly less famous, such as Thomas Fitzpatrick, James Clyman, and William Sublette.

Smith and his men fought their way through fierce rains, murderous rocky canyons, and bleak waterless plains. Smith had a hand-to-hand fight with a grizzly bear that nearly tore his face off, but it only briefly delayed the trek. In early 1824, they continued their struggle, running up against mountain blizzards, cold, and hunger. By March, they had located Sweetwater Creek through South Pass. They were the first men since Stuart to traverse the pass and find the trail along the creek that provided the easiest access.

Smith's expedition ranged through the mountains between the Snake and the Green rivers, which were now the center of the mountain fur trade. It was there that a new Hudson's Bay trader named Peter Skene Ogden countered the American threat with a "scorched-earth" policy — sending his men rampaging through the wilderness and clearing it of beaver. As furs grew scarcer, both Canadian and American

traders ranged farther south, and the exploration emphasis shifted to Wyoming and Utah.

Trappers continued for years to range the northwestern mountains, still finding enough beaver to justify the effort. But even in the 1820's, other people, not traders, developed an interest in the northwest. Ashley's reports on the South Pass and its environs naturally led to dreams of overland wagon trains and of settlers on the rich Oregon soil.

In the 1840's the Oregon Trail was used by early squatters moving into Oregon to homestead the land. And shortly thereafter, they began to clamor to Washington to give them territorial status. British Canada had hoped that the boundary would be drawn at the Columbia, but Canada had failed to follow up her fur traders with settlers. And she had failed to reckon with American Manifest Destiny, which by the 1840's anticipated the Stars and Stripes flying from Alaska all the way south to California. For by then American trail-breakers had forced their way into the Spanish southwest, had found it enticing, and had made all America hunger for it.

Above: a photograph of the 2,000-mile-long Oregon Trail, which looked much like this for miles of its length. It wound its way from Independence, Missouri, across prairies, deserts, and mountains to the northwest Pacific coast. It was the longest overland route used by settlers in their movement west. The deep ruts made by the wagon wheels can still be seen today. The covered wagons took six months to make the journey, often across flooded rivers, and with the ever-present threat of attack by Indians hanging over them. Always short of water and food, and facing the possibility of an outbreak of disease, the settlers' trek was a great feat of endurance.

Below: the Plaza and Church of El Paso. The largest city standing on the Mexico/United States border, El Paso (Spanish for "the pass") is known as the gateway to Mexico. Spanish priests founded a mission there in 1659, thus establishing an important Spanish foothold in the then-unexplored southwest territory.

The Road to Santa Fe

6

As traders rushed off up the Missouri once Lewis and Clark had shown the way, various entrepreneurs poured into the southwest in the footsteps of Zebulon Pike. Although the traders were aware of Pike's arrest and Spain's jealous protection of its mountain frontier, most of the adventurers seemed willing to take their chances—with varying consequences. In 1809, for instance, Anthony Glass reached as far as the upper Colorado River, in Texas, to trade with Indians, and returned to Missouri safely. In the same year, three traders named McLanahan, Smith, and Patterson tried to make a profit from the Indian trade on the Red River, but the Spanish came out and arrested them. And in 1812, another trio, Baird, Chambers, and McKnight, rode straight to Santa Fe with a pack train of trade goods. They were stopped by the Spanish and spent the next nine years in a Chihuahua jail. In 1814, a profit-seeker named Joseph Philibert took some trappers to the head of the Arkansas River to investigate the beaver population. They profited not only from the beaver skins but from buffalo hides as well. Fortunately, they were never bothered by the Spanish during their first hunting expeditions. But in 1816, the Spanish evidently thought that these Americans had been tapping Spanish resources for much too long, and proceeded to carry off Philibert and company to the Santa Fe prison. They were treated fairly leniently, however, and released in a few days.

In the words of one modern historian, Spain had dropped an "iron curtain" across the mountains in front of Santa Fe. They did not want trappers and traders to open the door for American expansionism. But this policy of isolationism only enhanced the American adventurers' desire to explore the Santa Fe region. The individual probes and thrusts might have continued for years if the Mexican revolt against Spain had not altered the situation.

Before that disruption, however, the United States and Spain had come to an agreement about the boundary of Louisiana. According to the Adams-Onis Treaty of 1819, the boundary line was to be drawn from the Sabine River northward to the Red. It would continue west along that river to 100° longitude, and then north to the Arkansas up to the 42nd parallel, which it followed to the Pacific. Because of this settlement, the United States decided that an official expedition ought to be conducted to bring back maps, charts, and descriptions of the natural resources of the area.

The decision to send troops to that area coincided with a wish to try out steamboats on the Missouri. As a result, in 1819, five poorly-built

Right: Karl Bodmer's "Unloading of the Steamboat *Yellowstone*, April 19, 1833." Steamboats were first used on the Missouri in the early 1800's and Stephen Long's experiments with these craft started what turned out to be a very successful method of transportation.

Right: these New Mexico religious statuettes of the 1800's were carved from wood and were used by the missionaries in their attempts to make Christian teaching more comprehensible to the Indians.

boats steamed off up the river with 1,000 men, while a sixth boat trailed behind bearing a handful of scientists under the command of Major Stephen Long. Unfortunately, the soldiers were inadequately supplied and began dying in their winter camp of scurvy, and assorted fevers. Major Long, however, took his scientists east again. It was there that he received his orders to take the group on a governmental scientific expedition into the southwest.

Long took with him some army topographers, a zoologist, a botanist, a naturalist, and an engraver named Samuel Seymour. Their main concern was to examine the terrain, the natural resources, and the wildlife. They were also to perform a fairly full exploration of the headwaters of the Red River, the United States' new southwestern extremity.

The group rode out along the Platte River in June 1820, and achieved a fairly quick crossing of the plains. By late June they had come within sight of the mountains. They continued to ride toward the mountains, proceeding southeast and then south along the South Platte.

The expedition continued south toward the Arkansas, still having explored no new ground. Balked by the mighty Royal Gorge of the upper Arkansas, the group split in two. A Captain Bell took some men down the Arkansas. Long took the others south in the direction of

the Red River. Bell's group entered Plains Indian territory—Arapaho, Kiowa, Cheyenne—and met harassment enough to drive three men to desertion. The deserters took with them most of the expedition's journals and scientific notes, and neither men nor papers were ever seen again. Meanwhile, Long marched across the Cimarron River and came upon a sizable waterway which he confidently identified as the Red. Following it east, the group underwent its first serious hardship, a scarcity of game that drove them to kill their horses for food. But in spite of their troubles, the men forged ahead. Eventually the river joined another waterway, which was clearly the Arkansas. Their time had been spent, then, following the Canadian River and not the Red.

In every way, Long's journey was a disaster. And he later compounded his failure by reiterating Pike's view of the central plains as the "Great American Desert... almost wholly unfit for cultivation." We may enjoy the irony that hindsight reveals. But some modern historians have pointed out that, in a sense, Long was right. The great plains *were* uncultivable in terms of the agricultural techniques employed in the United States at that time. In 1821, however, no one had time to listen to Stephen Long because of the upheavals in the Spanish southwest.

An American trader named William Becknell was fortunate enough

Above: a view of the chasm through which the Platte River issues from the Rocky Mountains. The Platte—in some places a mile wide—is the United States' shallowest river. It winds across central and southern Nebraska and was one of the main features of the settlers' route across the plains. The name Nebraska comes from the Oto Indian word "nebrathka," meaning flat water, the Indian name for the Platte.

to reap the benefits from that upheaval. He had organized a pack train
at Franklin, Missouri, which he led out across the plains to the great
bend of the Arkansas River. He headed west into Colorado, looking
for Indians to trade with, but instead was confronted by a detachment
of Spanish soldiers near the Canadian River. Becknell expected to be
arrested, but the soldiers told him that there had been a revolution.
They explained that the Spanish southwest was now independent
Mexico, and that the new nation welcomed (and needed) trade with
the United States. Becknell immediately headed toward Santa Fe,
sold his goods for huge profits in Mexican silver, and hurried back to
Franklin with the news.

Above: a Hopi Indian water bottle, of Spanish shape, but with Indian decoration. Water carriers such as this were very necessary to survival in the central plains, where scarcity of water was a continual problem.

In 1822, Becknell went out again. But this time he left the pack-horses at home and took wagons, the first wheels to roll onto the central plains. Osage Indians created some trouble in the journey's early days, and the wagon train was delayed in Kansas by floods. A wagon train usually consisted of about 25 wagons. Each could carry approximately 5,000 pounds weight. When Indians attacked, they could protect themselves, to some extent, by forming a circle to shield the livestock and provide a screen for the defenders. However, they were cumbersome vehicles and Becknell's main concern was finding a route through the mountains. For this reason, he diverged from his previous route from the upper Arkansas River and cut southwest across arid prairie,

hoping by this means to come to a more passable mountain gateway.

The wagon train went through unbearable days of blinding sun and heat. Their water gave out several times, and the mules began dropping one by one from thirst. Because of the men's own thirst, they resorted to drinking the dead mules' blood to keep themselves alive. But eventually Becknell's determination brought the exhausted party to the banks of the Cimarron River—which led almost due west to Santa Fe. Becknell achieved his goal and made his profits. But of prime importance was the fact that he had carved out the basic route to be used by traders and travelers for years to come—the Santa Fe Trail.

Legions of traders and trappers followed Becknell's wagon trail to Santa Fe in succeeding years. But the Americans had no sooner reached Santa Fe when they began looking farther west.

Etienne Provost may have been one of the first white men who entered the Great Salt Lake country of present-day Utah. In 1824, he worked his way up the Green River Valley and came to one of the small mountain rivers flowing into the Salt Lake. Whether he actually saw the lake is still debatable, even though he claimed to have done so.

Some historians seem to feel that the mountain man Jim Bridger was the first man to see the lake. In late 1824, when he had been trapping with a group near the Bear River, two trappers began to wonder where that river led. They sent young Bridger downstream to investigate. He arrived at a huge body of water, tasted it, and hurried back to announce that he had found an arm of the Pacific.

Bridger may have first tasted the Great Salt Lake, but it was Peter Skene Ogden, the Hudson's Bay Company's "Scourge of Oregon," who took the first thorough look at it. In December of 1828, after having explored unknown regions of Oregon and northern California, Ogden reached the shores of the Great Salt Lake. He explored the lakeshore to some extent, but of more importance, he moved through inhospitable desert to the west of the lake where he located a sizable western river. Ogden called it the Unknown, but today the river is known as the Humboldt. Its valley was to form one of the major highways to California and the Pacific coast.

In the late 1820's, both Jedediah Smith and Ogden went farther afield into the desolate terrain of Utah, and separately, both explorers reached down through the mountains into the badlands of Arizona. Eventually they went their own ways, westward into the heart of California.

Above: the Great Salt Lake, Utah. Though fed by freshwater streams, the lake is very salty. This is due to the high rate of evaporation and the fact that the lake is extremely shallow.

Right: frontiersman Jim Bridger. Hunter, trapper, trader, and guide, he was possibly the first to see the Great Salt Lake, and the first man in the Yellowstone area. He became a semilegendary figure in the West.

Reaching for California
7

By the middle of the 1800's three routes penetrated through the southwestern mountains into the promised land of California. Basically they followed old Indian trails or Spanish routes which still required rediscovery by Americans. The first route to be established—called the Old Spanish Trail—emerged from the determination of Jedediah Smith, the enthusiastic young mountain man who was second to none in his eagerness to explore the land about him. Smith's trapping journeys in southern Idaho and northern Utah made him keen to press on into the unknown regions of the southwest in the hope of finding unexploited trapping country, and possibly setting up new trade routes to California and from there into the Pacific northwest. In August, 1826, he and 15 trappers went to investigate the area.

The group moved along the Wasatch Mountains to the Sevier and Virgin rivers. The going became difficult as they had to drag themselves through a dry, dusty land that Smith called a land of starvation. Pushing on to the Colorado River, they followed it southward through the starkly rugged Black Mountain region of Arizona. By now the struggle was for survival. Their horses weakened and died, and the men resorted to eating the leathery flesh.

Then suddenly they emerged out of desolation and into plenty—the green fields of the Mojave Indians near what is now Davis Dam. The Indians made them welcome and helped the explorers regain their strength during a two-week stay. The men learned that California lay nearby, and Smith had no hesitation in going on. In November, with Mojave guides, the party crossed the Mojave Desert on an ancient Indian trail that led into and through the San Bernardino Mountains. They became the first Americans to enter California overland.

Smith arrived at San Gabriel (now part of Los Angeles), and then went on to San Diego to meet the governor. The Spanish authorities were not pleased with this new American break-through, but they let the Americans depart without interruption in January, 1827. Smith's party moved out north to the San Bernardino Valley, and then went on to the San Joaquin Valley. By spring they were in northern Cali-

Left: Jedediah Smith, American
trader and explorer, who set
out from the Great Salt Lake to find
trade routes to California. This
picture shows him crossing the
desert from Green River to the
Spanish settlement at San Gabriel.

Above: sketch by William Rich Hutton showing San Gabriel, Los Angeles, in 1847. Los Angeles was the second village established by the Spanish in California and when Jim Bridger and his party arrived there in 1826 they were not welcomed by the Spaniards, who saw the Americans' arrival as a threat to their control. Mexico took over government of Los Angeles in 1822 and American naval forces captured it in 1846.

Above right: the Great Basin, a desolate, waterless valley in the Nevada desert. This arid, infertile area is true desert, entirely different from the "Great American Desert" which Pike and Long said was uncultivable, but which has become the great farmland of the United States.

fornia. Smith tried to cross the still snow-clogged passes of the High Sierra, but killed five horses in the attempt, and very nearly killed his men. He finally left some of them in a camp to wait for a thaw, and with two others forced his way over the mountains. After the long journey, they approached the vast Nevada desert called the Great Basin.

The three men decided to cross the desert. Had they known the hardship to be faced, they might have decided otherwise. The hot glare of the sun and the desolation were unbearable. Several of the horses that had survived the mountain passes weakened and died in the desert. The men were again forced to eat horsemeat and the few stringy, desert rabbits they could catch. Their water ran out. One of the men lay down to die. But Smith and the other man went on until, at last, they stumbled upon a waterhole. Revived, they returned for their companion, and the three of them somehow managed to stagger forward. After 20 days of desert travel they arrived, in late June, at the exact spot that they had left the previous year—the south shore of the Great Salt Lake.

The fact that Smith arrived at his exact destination shows his remarkable sense of direction. He had no instruments, no guides from San Gabriel onward, and no trails of any kind to follow. Yet he had circled through the California interior and had come over the most inhospitable mountains and the widest desert in America.

Smith also demonstrated the mountain man's stamina and restlessness by setting off again, after only 10 days in camp, to meet the men left behind in California. With 18 men, he followed more or less the same route southward to the Mojave villages. But when they reached those villages, they found that the situation had changed. Since their last visit, the Indians had fought with a party of white trappers from Taos, with the result that the Indians turned hostile toward Smith and his men as well. When Smith's party began a crossing of the Colorado River, the Mojaves attacked, killing 10 men and leaving Smith and the other 8 stranded on a makeshift raft in midstream. But the stranded men safely crossed the river and escaped into the desert, where Smith led them back to his old route and the Mojave River. They went northward, and reached the mouth of the Sacramento River where they struggled through the wilderness along its banks in order to winter in the Sacramento Valley. In June, 1828, they found themselves in Oregon, where they trapped along the Umpqua River.

One day Smith and two men took a canoe to reconnoiter up a nearby stream. In their absence, a band of forest Indians brutally massacred every man in the camp but one. The survivor fled through the forest, and Smith and his two men fled as well. All four eventually reached the Hudson's Bay Company's Fort Vancouver.

Below: a water canteen made of ribbed metal, now rusty, dating from about 1860. This was probably used in the Civil War, but is almost certainly like those carried earlier in the century, which would have been used by people like Jed Smith.

Below: Fort Vancouver, built in 1825 on the Columbia River, near the mouth of the Willamette (opposite today's Portland), as the Pacific headquarters of the Hudson's Bay Company. Surrounded by a stockade 318 feet square, the fort consisted of warehouses, stores, offices, dormitories, a brick powder magazine, and a dock for ocean-going ships. There were herds of livestock, grainfields, and orchards. To Jed Smith, on his arrival there in 1828, the fort was a symbol of the great power of the Hudson's Bay Company, which he called "all grasping."

From the Fort, the group made their way north, almost to the present Canadian border. They trapped as they went. By 1830, they had returned to their own territory around Wind River.

That year, Smith retired from the fur trade to farm in Missouri. In 1831, though, he decided to try one more trek into the West. This time he went with a wagon train going to trade in Santa Fe. On the Cimarron Cutoff, Smith rode out alone to look for water and was attacked by a band of Comanche. In true western fashion, he accounted for the Indian chief before he was killed.

Smith's achievements were not merely adventures. He is remembered not as an Indian-fighter, but as a brilliant explorer. He penetrated unknown wilderness and mapped and reported on much of the ground he covered. In this way he vastly extended the United States' knowledge of and appetite for its riches. In addition, Smith

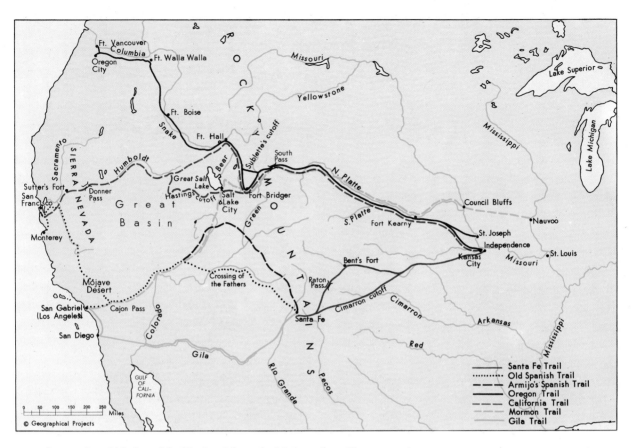

Above: The western trails that first the explorers and then the settlers followed on their way west. Some of the trails were established by individuals or groups — such as the Mormon Trail — but others, like the Old Spanish Trail, were traditional routes that had been used for years.

carved out the Old Spanish Trail, although Mojave hostility caused the route to be altered later.

By the early 1830's, the southerly overland links between Santa Fe and California had been completed. The making of the Gila Trail by James Pattie and Ewing Young and the alteration of the Old Spanish Trail by William Wolfskill opened the way southwest. The trappers and traders were the first arrivals of the American influx that was yet to come to California. Before that wave of settlers took place, though, the special routes of the trappers had to be developed out in the east.

This process of opening up routes was a slow one. The old routes used by the mountain men had almost to be *re*discovered, and official fact-finding explorations to be organized. For example, the South Pass into the Green River Valley offered a perfect wagon route to both Oregon and California. But as yet no one had defined the easiest and quickest way from the pass into California's unpopulated central valleys. Settlers could never have traversed the difficult southern trails laid down by Smith and Pattie. And, unfortunately, no one had located a better, more northerly route.

A start had been made, however, in 1828, when Peter Skene Ogden found the Humboldt River. The next year Ogden retraced his steps to the Humboldt, cut across a portion of the Great Basin, and pushed south to the Colorado River. When he eventually reached the Colorado, he then took his men along the river to the Gulf of California, and so became the first white man to cross the American West from north to

Above: trappers and Indians forming
a cavalcade. Groups such as this
opened up the footpath trails of
the mountain men and made them
negotiable by the settlers.

south. But he did not leave a complete trail behind him. He left only
the beginning of one, following the Humboldt River.

Two years later, the government sent out an army captain named
Benjamin Bonneville to have a good look at the settlement possibil-
ities beyond the mountains, disguising his researches as fur trading.
Bonneville produced little new knowledge about the Indians or the
terrain. However, he did contribute indirectly to the opening up of
the Far West. In 1832 he set out with 110 men from his post on the
Green River on an exploring expedition into California. One of the
party was Tennessee frontiersman Joseph Reddeford Walker, who
later established the basic settler route into California.

The party traveled west from the Salt Lake to the marshy headwaters
of the Humboldt River, as Ogden had done. At that point, they had a
brush with some Digger Indians, killing many of them. The Diggers
had gathered in great numbers, but the trigger-happy explorers did
not wait to find out if they were really hostile or merely curious.

After this far-from-noble victory, Walker's party moved into the
mountains, probably up the Walker River, over the Divide into what
is now Yosemite National Park. As usual, heavy snow in the Sierra
made for a grueling passage. But conditions improved as the party
made the descent into California. They were the first white men to see
and describe the Yosemite Valley, the giant redwoods, and the general
richness of the land. By December, 1833, Walker and his companions

were standing on the coast of the Pacific south of San Francisco Bay.

The expedition began the journey back in February, and this time Walker moved through the San Joaquin Valley, where he discovered the low-altitude gap through the southern Sierra to be named "Walker Pass." It was a vital discovery because it completed a suitable route for settlers, which came to be called the California Trail.

Meanwhile, more and more Americans were using the Old Spanish and Gila trails to reach California. Others, particularly those who had already established shipping companies on the coast, traveled by sea. And in the late 1830's, traders regularly moved in and out of California from Santa Fe, thus emphasizing the United States' presence. Many of these Americans settled in California, which at that time belonged to Mexico. Although the settlers proclaimed loyalty to Mexico, they did, in fact, form a nucleus of United States' expansion. Several of the settlers managed to obtain land grants from Mexico. Swiss-born John

Right: watercolor by Alfred Jacob Miller, painted in 1837, of Captain Joseph Reddeford Walker, the Tennessee frontiersman who established the route for settlers traveling to California. He is followed—at the correct distance dictated by etiquette—by his Indian wife.

Sutter was given a huge area in the Sacramento Valley, where he established a fort. Near Sutter's Fort was the enormous ranch of John Marsh, another new "Mexican" and a fugitive from justice in the east.

These establishments, and others like them, were in some of the richest land in the west. In addition they were far away from the eyes of the Mexican authorities. News of such properties reached the Missouri frontier and groups of pioneers gathered to launch a small-scale invasion of California.

The first group from Missouri crossed the prairies in 1841. It consisted of 69 people, including women and children, and was organized for the journey by John Bartleson and John Bidwell of Missouri. The mountain man Thomas Fitzpatrick guided their wagon train, which was made up of 14 covered wagons and a number of assorted carts. They traveled along the Platte River and through South Pass to the Bear River Valley. There, in August, part of the group split off and headed for Oregon. About 30 remained intent on making for California, among them Nancy Kelsey, the 18-year-old wife of Benjamin Kelsey, and their baby daughter. They were the only woman and child to complete the journey overland.

They set off without maps or guides to the region, leaving Fitzpatrick to go his own way. Having exchanged their wagons for pack animals they found themselves stumbling around in the desert of the Salt Lake region for weeks, subsisting on mule meat and coyotes. At

Left: San Francisco as it would have looked to Joseph Walker and his party when they arrived in 1833. The Bay was located by Gaspar de Portolá in 1769. The first settlers arrived in 1776, and later that year the Spaniards founded the Mission San Francisco de Asis (later renamed Mission Dolores). The village that grew, El Paraje de Yerba Buena (the little valley of the good herb), was taken by the Americans in 1846 and a year later was named San Francisco.

Above: the sort of Mexican ranch owner who would have formed a large part of the population of California in the 1800's. His clothes were elaborate. The cape, called a manga, is an oval of blue or green material, lined with painted percale (fine, closely-woven cotton). The velvet collar is overlaid with gold lace, and a gold fringe decorates the shoulder. His hat is of Vicuña felt decorated with gold lace. His chamois vest reveals a shirt of fine fabric pleated at the front.

last the party reached the Humboldt River. There some Indians gave them vague directions, and the company moved into the mountains. Hardship, caused in part by ignorance, continued to test their endurance, but the pioneers were determined to go on. The expedition went too far south before crossing the Sierra, but finally made its way along the Walker River and through the high mountain passes. Emerging in late October into intractable canyon country, they almost despaired of ever reaching California. But still they pushed on, and after a few days their perseverance was rewarded. They descended into the greenery of the San Joaquin Valley. Many of them, like Marsh, were able to acquire land from Mexico.

One of the party, Joseph Chiles, returned to Missouri for more emigrants, and led a large party westward in 1843. Chiles took some of them on a circuitous route northwest into Oregon and then swung down into California. But he did not find a better route that way. In 1843, Joseph Walker led a wagon train via the Humboldt River to find Walker Pass, although they had to abandon the wagons in order to cross it. But in 1844, a group at last took covered wagons all the way from Missouri to California.

That group contained some 40 people, including 8 women and 15 children. It was led by Elisha Stevens and guided by at least two mountain men. One of the guides found a shorter route from South Pass to the Bear River, known as Sublette's Cutoff. From the Bear, the party

Above: the Sierra Nevada, the range of mountains which forms the eastern boundary of California. After many weary months of travel across desert and plain, the pioneers were faced with these mountains to cross. Wagon trains followed the trails blazed by trappers and explorers, widening them to make a way possible. Many of them failed and the early trails were littered with signs of their failure. It was never easy to get a loaded wagon through the steep and rocky passes.

entered Idaho and rested at a fur-trade post. In mid-August, they went south to rejoin Walker's California Trail at the Humboldt River. An old Indian told them about a useful pass to the west—some distance away from Walker's southbound route. The new route led to the two-day horror of the Forty Mile Desert between Humboldt Sink and Carson River in Nevada. This tract of land was strewn with dead animals' stinking, rotting flesh, and was littered with abandoned wagons, cooking pots, camping equipment, and anything that trappers had discarded to lighten their loads. They moved on to Truckee River, and traveled through the location where present-day Reno, Nevada, is situated. With winter coming on and food running short, the party struggled up into the mountains.

After laboring with the oxen and the laden wagons up mountain slopes and battling across icy, rock-strewn streams they found the

pass Indians had told them about. It was barely traversable by wagons. They might have turned back had it not been for Stevens' leadership and the party's high morale. But by early December, the wagons were through the mountain corridor and into California near Sutter's Fort.

It was the first time that a wagon train had crossed the continent into California. But this great achievement in surviving the long trek, and the importance of discovering the pass, were overshadowed by the tragic fate of the Donner party in the same pass in 1846-47. The party was badly organized and rife with dissension among its members. They were caught by early snowfalls in the California Sierra and forced to camp there. Food ran out and it is thought some members resorted to cannibalism. And today that vital gateway to the Californian valleys is called Donner Pass, commemorating the grisly failure rather than the heroic success.

Above: a typical pioneer family with their wagons. Most of the men and women who pushed the frontiers westward were simple people who faced the hardships and privations because they wanted a chance to improve their lives in the virgin lands of the West. Frontiersmen had to be farmers, hunters, and trappers, handy with an ax and able to build a shelter, boat, wagon, or sledge, and to mend a broken plow. Their lives were hard and the rewards were seldom great for the first settlers.

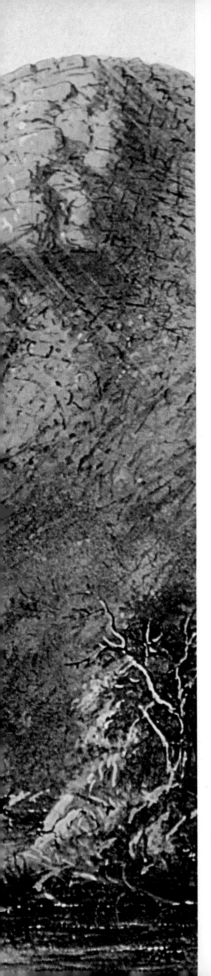

"The Pathfinder"
8

During the early 1840's American expansion rapidly increased. Droves of American adventurers and settlers moved west along the Oregon Trail or over the Sierra on the California Trail, while Britain and Mexico watched helplessly. Britain's hands were tied by an agreement that established joint Anglo-American occupation of Oregon, with a boundary settlement yet to be made. The British at first had hoped that the boundary would eventually follow the Columbia River. But the Hudson's Bay Company soon grew pessimistic and anticipated that the Americans would settle into territory beyond that line. For this reason, in 1843, the Hudson's Bay Company built a new Pacific headquarters on Vancouver Island to be assured of their hold in the area. That same year, 1,000 Americans moved into Oregon, calling themselves the "Great Immigration." A sizable number had invaded the valleys of California, too, and the Mexican authorities had become sufficiently dependent on American trade to forestall any anti-American moves.

From then on, American exploration became almost exclusively an explicit investigation of the Oregon and California regions prior to their takeover. The War Department had formed a Corps of Topographical Engineers for this purpose. Among them was a young lieutenant named John Charles Frémont, whose travels were to earn him the title of "the Pathfinder."

Frémont was a handsome, energetic, and romantic figure. He had a way with the ladies and a flair for publicity, but he also had well-defined qualities of leadership that attracted the loyalty of the roughest

Left: the "Devil's Gate," a notable landmark on the Oregon Trail, where the Sweetwater River—a branch of the North Platte—flows through a ridge of granite mountains.

Right: John Charles Frémont (1813–1890), American soldier, explorer, and politician. He became known as "the Pathfinder" during the course of his explorations of the greater part of the country between the Rockies and the Pacific coast. Frémont was the first Republican candidate to be nominated for the presidency in 1856 but he was defeated by Buchanan by 60 electoral votes.

Above: map, published by R. H. Laurie in 1830, showing the "Probable Course" of the Buenaventura River. This mythical river was regularly shown on maps of this period because people believed that such a river *should* be there. The fact that anyone who had traveled there knew quite well that it was not, made little or no difference.

of mountain men. Frémont had gained his first exploring experience around the Mississippi. He had done such a good job that he was chosen by Senator Thomas Hart Benton as the leader of a large-scale exploration west of the mountains.

In 1842, Frémont went into Oregon in the company of a cartographer named Charles Preuss and a handful of mountain men, including Kit Carson. They broke no new ground, except when Frémont climbed one of the Wind River mountains to perform the symbolic act of planting the American flag.

The next year, Frémont took his mapmaker and his mountain men (Thomas Fitzpatrick as well as Carson) on a careful investigation of Oregon, as far as the coast. His instructions, which referred to "the interior of *our* continent," made it clear that the exploration was to define the best areas for further American settlement. They discovered many promising areas, taking special note of the Bear River Valley and finding suitable territory in the environs of the Great Salt Lake. From the lake, Frémont moved by way of the Snake River up to the Columbia to complete his task. Then he impulsively exceeded his orders when he decided to go south to look for that mythical river, the Buena-ventura (believed to link the Pacific and the Salt Lake, and placed on most maps of the west in spite of the fact that no one had ever seen it).

With the rapid approach of winter, the expedition set out in November and moved south to the Deschutes River. Within a short time, they were struggling up the slopes of western mountains in the first deep snowfalls of December, and inching down rugged terrain to enter the Great Basin of Nevada. Cutting across its western edge, they began (near Lake Tahoe) a foolhardy winter assault on the Sierra Nevada.

Driving snow, fog, and interminable rocky slopes would have been bad enough, but Frémont complicated his ascent by dragging along a small cannon that he had begged from the Army to impress the Indians. The group's horses and mules weakened, their supplies ran low, and their Indian guide deserted. Feet froze, eyes were blinded from snow-glare, men collapsed from hunger, and one man went mad. But Frémont drove them on, and by mid-February they had crossed the Divide. They continued the struggle through heavy snow and dangerous mountain terrain until they emerged into the "perpetual spring," as Frémont called it, of the Sacramento Valley.

In March, they left that valley, where they had recuperated at Sutter's Fort, and moved south through the San Joaquin Valley in order to cross the Sierra through the Tehachapi Pass. They continued south to the Old Spanish Trail and turned east, where they met Joseph Walker, whose mountain skills eased their passage the rest of the way to the Sevier River and eastward into Colorado.

Frémont wrote a brilliant report of this epic journey, and Preuss drew up the maps of it. It was widely circulated in the east, and had enormous influence over would-be emigrants. Frémont may not have located many easy or tempting paths, but he fully awakened the spirit of Manifest Destiny. In 1844, President James K. Polk was elected

Below: an Indian guide presenting a prospective employer with his "certificate." The success, or otherwise, of an exploratory mission depended largely on the skill and reliability (or lack of it) of the Indian guides. Their certificates were probably no more than a letter from a previously satisfied customer.

on the platform of expanding Oregon all the way north to Alaska ("54° 40' or Fight"). And in 1846, the United States successfully managed to pick a fight with Mexico in order to launch an expansionist war. Frémont, as it turned out, helped to promote that war.

In 1845, he was sent west again to make surveys of the Arkansas and Red rivers, and to examine the Salt Lake region and much of the Sierra Nevada for useful military routes in case of war. He assigned a young lieutenant to make a survey of the rivers while he plunged back into the southwestern mountains, accompanied by Kit Carson, Joe Walker, and a tough contingent of soldiers and mountain men. His route led them through the Tennessee Pass, across the Grand River, and along the White River to the Great Salt Lake. From there they marched across the wastes of the Great Basin to Walker Lake. Frémont then took some of the party southwest to the Donner Pass, while Joe Walker guided the others southward to cross the Sierra at Walker Pass.

Frémont arrived at Sutter's Fort in California in December, having found the Sierra unusually open and free of snow. He had located a useful and reasonably quick route into the Californian interior, and lost no time in reporting it to the American consul in Monterey. But routes were to be the least important result of this entry into California.

Mexico was alive with the talk of war. Texas had already been snapped up by the United States' annexation in 1845, and the Mexicans feared that California could easily be taken in the same way. Understandably, the Californian authorities objected to the presence of Frémont and his 60 well-armed men. As a result, in February, 1846, Monterey's General Castro ordered Frémont out of California. The Pathfinder fortified himself on Hawk's Peak and dared the Mexicans to make him go. But after a few days without being troubled, Frémont and his men slipped away by night, heading north for Oregon.

At about that time, General Zachary Taylor and his troops had massed near the Rio Grande, hoping to tempt Mexico into striking the first blow. Sure enough, in May, 1846, Mexico succumbed to temptation, killed some of Taylor's dragoons, and started the war.

Meanwhile, a group of American rebels who had no idea that the war had started began a revolt of their own. In June, they took over Mexican headquarters in Sonoma. They celebrated their success by raising a makeshift flag picturing a bear over the words "California Republic." This event came to be known as the Bear Flag Revolt.

The real conquest of California, though, was conducted by Frémont and General Stephen Kearny. Frémont marched south at the head of 150 mountain men and American pioneers, while Kearny effortlessly took New Mexico with his motley Army of the West. Eventually, Frémont's revolutionaries joined forces with the United States military, and by January, 1847, California was American. Frémont was named as the first governor of this new United States acquisition.

The United States had now managed to acquire the southwest and the northwest, which enlarged its territory immensely. Settlers by the hundreds poured through South Pass each year, branching out to the north and the south. They were not deterred by the Indian men-

Above: James Knox Polk (1795–1849), 11th President of the United States from 1845–1849, when territorial growth was at its height. During his term the Star-Spangled Banner was raised over Texas and most of what are now the nine western states.

Right: map showing the Far West, with the routes of the trappers, the mountain men, and explorers who mapped the area west of the Rocky Mountains.

Above: while General Kearny took New Mexico, American forces under General Zachary Taylor went into Mexico itself. Here American troops storm the bishop's palace in Monterrey, in a drawing by a private in the army, Samuel Chamberlain.

ace in Oregon, nor by postwar dislocations in California. They were not distressed by the tales of the Hastings and Donner parties, both of which had suffered terribly in their attempts to reach California.

In 1846-47, Brigham Young translated Frémont's glowing words into the reality of the Mormon migration to the Salt Lake. The Mormons were followers of a new religion they claimed was based on revelation. They had been surrounded by hostile neighbors in Illinois and Missouri, who had eventually shot their original leader and burned their towns and houses to the ground. The Mormons traveled across the plains ignorant of frontier rigors but unswervingly determined to make the desert bloom. They hoped to gain a worthwhile

Right: war was declared between the United States and Mexico in May, 1846, but in June of that year a band of American settlers, not knowing that war had been declared, staged the Bear Flag Revolt. After capturing the fort at Sonoma, Mexico's headquarters in northern California, they raised this flag—a homemade banner, bearing a star, a grizzly bear, and the words "Californian Republic."

home of their own which would be located a long way from eastern persecutors. Because of this hope, many Mormons starved, froze, and crippled themselves during the long journey "home."

Elsewhere, in Oregon and California, the living was easier, and the wagon trains kept plodding across the prairies. This increased the populations of those regions considerably, but the great determining factor that flooded the west with swarms of newcomers was the gold found in the mountains of California.

The frenzy began in early 1848, when a man helping to build a saw-mill on the property of John Sutter noticed a sparkle of yellow in a mountain stream. Throughout the spring, various workers scraped up bits of the yellow stuff, tested it, and proved it was gold. In May, the traditional cry went up in San Francisco, "gold in them thar hills!" By June, the city had been virtually deserted, and the news was spreading east like a prairie fire. All of California seemed to be grubbing in the Sierra foothills. Oregonians left hard-won homesteads and hurried south for their share. In the beginning of 1849, thousands of easterners mortgaged their futures to pay profiteering ships' passage fees to California. Many thousands more pinned their hopes on the overland trails. One estimate numbers the overlanders in 1849 at 50,000. Most of them were channeled through the South Pass and were directed by hastily written guide books that seldom mentioned the hazards to be

Above: Brigham Young (1801—1877), the Mormon who led his followers from Illinois to Utah when anti-Mormonism forced them to leave first one place, then another. They reached the Great Salt Lake valley in 1847.

Right: a facsimile of an entry in the diary of William Bigler, who was at Sutter's Mill, California, when gold was discovered. Bigler was a member of the Mormon Church, working his way from Los Angeles to the Church's new home at Utah in 1848. He had reached Sacramento where he was employed by John Sutter when the first nuggets of gold were found by James Marshall.

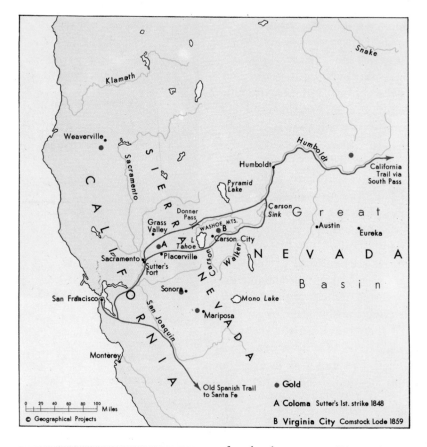

Right: details from "Grant and His Generals" by Balling, showing Generals Devin, Custer, and Kilpatrick. Although Custer (detail at top) is shown as a Civil War general, his greatest fame came as an Indian-fighter, and especially through his famous Last Stand on the Little Bighorn River, where Custer and his entire regiment were killed by the Sioux.

Above: the California gold rush brought many different nationalities to the shores of America. This engraving shows a Chinese man going to the mines in 1853.

faced—deserts, warlike Indians, or the difficult mountain pathways.

The struggles and miseries of the "forty-niners," as they were called, have only minor relevance to western exploration. Most of them followed the settlers' trails as best they could. Others blithely decided on Jed Smith's Old Spanish Trail, and met the greater horrors of the Mojave Desert and other neighboring wastelands. One group discovered a blazing basin below sea level, walled in by mountains seemingly without exits. They called this basin Death Valley. A more useful discovery was made by a company of Mormons trekking eastward from their successful gold diggings. They located a pass through the Sierra along the Carson River that neatly linked the goldfields (Placerville especially) with the Humboldt River headwaters. This route and, to some extent, the Donner Pass, became the most popular for gold-seeking emigrants during the rush.

The Californian gold rush reached its peak in 1852, by which time the mountains seemed overrun with men of every nationality, including a major influx of Chinese. The miners began to scatter through the mountains in the 1850's, hoping to find a repetition of the rich veins of California. They risked Apache attacks along the Gila River and eastward into Arizona. They then filtered into Nevada, up unknown rivers and canyons, digging and panning along the way. Their searches were rewarded by the fantastic wealth of the Comstock Lode near Virginia City, Nevada, on the edge of the Great Basin.

Exploration, of course, continued to be incidental and haphazard, but new western regions began to open up when precious metals were found in their soils. Miners fanned out later into Colorado, into British Columbia in the famous Cariboo rush of the 1860's, and eventually into more northerly states such as Montana and the Dakotas. As late as 1874, gold turned up in the Black Hills of South Dakota. Although this area had been crossed before, it was given a thorough, scientific survey by an expedition under the leadership of Colonel George Armstrong Custer. The expedition was typical of the general overrunning of the west by engineers, topographers, and surveyors, who were busily seeking out the small unknown areas that remained. Their work was often difficult, but the unknown areas were now linked by established trails and outposts. The blank frontier was vanishing, and a more complete picture of the west was being built up.

The Fact-finders
9

As western gold created something of a population explosion and Americans rushed westward in hundreds of thousands, the United States wanted to know more about the newest additions to its transcontinental nation. Those early settlers also began yearning for better links with home than dusty prairie trails and cruel mountain passes. As a result, the era of exploration of the 1800's ended with the same kind of government-backed, fact-finding expeditions that had begun it.

Some of these parties went looking for improved routes for settlers, with an eye to transcontinental communications. Others went to perform scientific surveys of the wilderness. By the late 1840's, the days of original discovery were past. Any discoveries yet to be made were incidental and comparatively trivial—a small river, a low range of hills, or a useful mountain pass. But even though the scientists and surveyors were not discoverers, they were still important explorers. For their comprehensive and systematic examination of the West formed a necessary prelude to its wholesale settlement.

Oddly enough, even before stagecoaches had begun operating routes into California, and before the steam locomotive had lost the sheen of novelty in the East, Americans began talking about transcontinental railroads. Many put their words into action by looking for routes. In mid-winter 1848–1849, Frémont organized a party to scour the mountains for a usable pass. But the fierce snows accounted for the loss of 10 men and doomed this last pathfinding attempt to failure.

The army (i.e. the Topographical Engineers) instigated other searches for routes in the Gila River region and the plains of west Texas. Similar teams looked in New Mexico, while Captain Howard Stansbury examined the Salt Lake region and the Mormon settlements, locating the valuable Cheyenne Pass. Much of Stansbury's route eventually formed the path of the Union Pacific Railroad, but no one paid much attention to it at the time (1850). Railroad plans had become excuses for eastern financial and political machinations. No one was really ready to build a line, and so geographical facts tended to be ignor-

Left: prospectors washing gold from the Calaveras River in northern central California. The "forty-niners," as these men were called, flocked to California from all over the world and by the end of 1849, the population of California had increased from 20,000 to over 107,000.

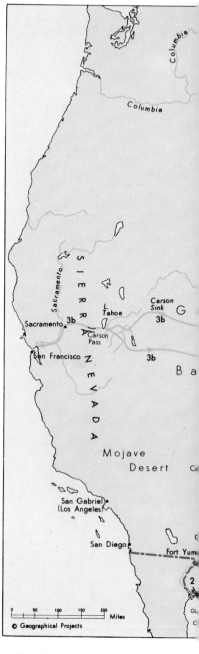

Above: a 50-foot linen measuring tape, with book-form leather carrying case, which also holds a note pad and pencil, as used by the surveyors in the 1800's.

Left: a prismatic compass by Andrew Yeates. Made in the late 1800's, this instrument has a spirit level, a small telescope, and a tripod clamp. These allow more accurate bearings to be taken.

ed. Surveyors were still looking for railroad routes in the early 1860's.

Before then, the army began a series of surveying expeditions into the West, called, by the historian William H. Goetzmann, the "Great Reconnaissance." Some of these centered on Utah because of the Mormon War of 1857, a war set off when the Mormon church clashed with the federal government over who really ruled the territory. As a by-product, Lieutenant J. C. Ives made a notable exploration along part of the Colorado River, though the river's extent remained a mystery for years. In 1859, Captain J. N. Macomb systematically explored the wilderness northwest of Santa Fe, emerging eventually into the Green River Valley with the first clear idea of that region's drainage. Captain

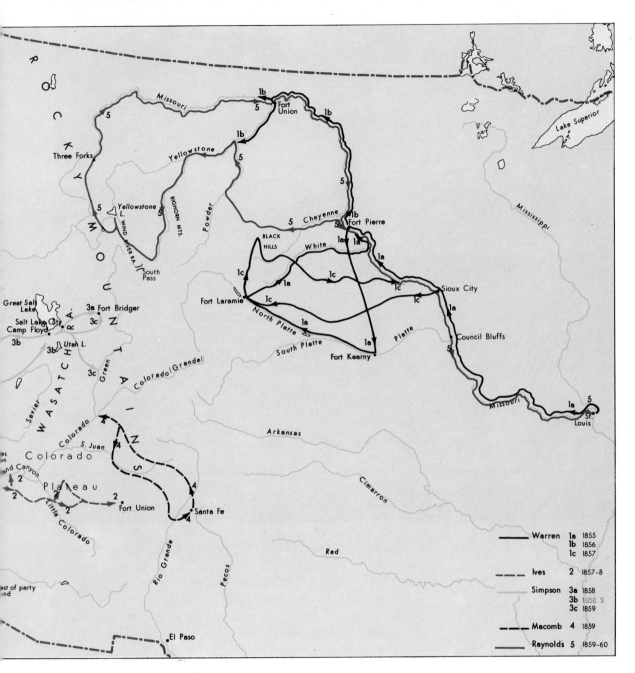

Above: routes of the surveyors Warren, Ives, Simpson, Macomb, and Raynolds, who worked out the details of the topography of the western United States.

J. H. Simpson roamed the Great Basin and the Wasatch Mountains. Lieutenant G. K. Warren made an overland foray into the Dakotas, partly to find military routes for operations against the Sioux. Captain W. F. Raynolds wandered the Wind River region looking for a southern access into the rugged terrain of what is now Yellowstone Park. He failed to find one, even with the expert guidance of Jim Bridger.

At about the same period, the British began to show interest in the Canadian west. The Hudson's Bay Company seemed doubtful whether the Canadian west was suitable for settlers, but its view could hardly be called objective. For this reason, in 1857, Britain sent Captain John Palliser and some scientists to examine the Canadian west.

Palliser's topographical reports were praiseworthy, but, oddly enough, he returned with the strongest warning about the aridity of the prairies, or the Great Canadian Desert. This attitude to the American plains, as put forward by Pike and Stephen Long, had already been discredited by Frémont and others. Revaluations of Canada's magnificent wheat-growing areas had yet to be made.

And so inquiries into the West continued. Reports cascaded onto government desks, with maps of exceptional accuracy accompanying them. Frémont's map of this route in 1843-44 was the first map to represent the western regions comprehensively. But Lieutenant Warren's map of the entire trans-Mississippi west (completed in 1857) took the prize for accuracy and comprehensiveness. Reports of scientific observations became as numerous as those of the topographical explorations. Geologists rushed to the West, and many became involved in examining the stratified canyons of Colorado. Paleontologists joined them after John Evans returned from South Dakota with a treasure-hoard of fossils. Botanists and zoologists scattered across the wilderness to study plants and animals. Archeologists searched among the leftovers of prehistoric tribes, mainly in New

Left: an illustration from Howard Stansbury's "An expedition to the valley of the Great Salt Lake of Utah," published in Philadelphia in 1852, showing surveyors setting up a baseline station in the Utah desert.

Below: Captain John Palliser, one of the scientists sent by Britain to make a topographical examination of the Canadian west in 1857.

Mexico. The West, then, became filled with excited and eager scientists.

One of the busiest groups concentrated on the mountain-strewn terrain of the southwest. Led by Josiah D. Whitney, from 1860 onward, the California Survey made a massive assault on that region's geology. Its scientists encountered the dramas of mountain exploration—such as floods, snows, and crippling cold. Many of these explorer-geologists became expert mountain climbers. Whitney and company inched up to the 14,162-foot summit of Mount Shasta, in 1862, where they nearly collapsed from lack of oxygen. A dynamic Yale graduate named Clarence King joined them in 1863, and attempted to stand "on the top of California." With only a bowie knife, a geologist's hammer, and a rawhide lasso, King ascended Mount Tyndall and climbed within a few hundred feet of the region's great peak, Mount Whitney, so named for Josiah Whitney.

Meanwhile, far to the east, the Confederacy's secession had launched the war between the States. Congress was now northern-controlled, so that it could overcome some of the sectional politics that had blocked a decision on a transcontinental railroad. An engineer named Theodore D. Judah had located what seemed to be a useful route through the

Left: Pueblo Indians and their dwellings. These are modern descendants of the ancient Pueblo tribes, who still live in much the same way as their forefathers.

Sierra. And though it was to be some years before a comparable route could be found through the Rockies, the transcontinental railroad got under way in 1862. The Central Pacific was to build over the Sierra, and the Union Pacific was to cross the plains and the Rockies to join the Central. (By the mid-1860's several smaller railroad lines were criss-crossing the Midwest.) The two lines were built in frantic competition. The Union Pacific only caught up when, in 1865, a young engineer named James Evans located an ideal pass through the Rockies, near present-day Cheyenne, Wyoming.

By 1869, California had its steel link with the east, and in the 1870's and 1880's, other railroad companies rushed to throw their competitive lines across the mountains—the Kansas Pacific, Texas Pacific, Southern Pacific, Northern Pacific and, of course, the Atchison, Topeka, and Santa Fe. By then, too, newly confederated Canada was dreaming of transcontinental rails. It spent much of the 1870's looking for a route across the fearsome topography north of Lake Superior, and across the jagged Canadian Rockies. The railroad engineer Sandford Fleming led hosts of surveys in these inhospitable regions. By 1880, the

Right: a rawhide lasso, the frontiersman's most valuable and versatile tool, was used for anything and everything, from catching cattle and pulling wagons over muddy swamps, to killing a snake or tying a pack.

Left: by the 1860's a transcontinental railroad had been started, with two companies working toward each other—the Central Pacific across the Sierra, the Union Pacific across the plains and the Rockies. This picture shows the workmen building the track across the Nevada desert in 1868.

Right: the Canadian Rockies, showing the terrain through which the Canadian Pacific railroad engineers forced their steel link with the West.

Canadian Pacific Railway began construction. It overcame monumental financial obstacles thanks to the business genius of its president, George Stephen. And it overcame constructional obstacles because of the American railroad manager William Van Horne, its general manager. He believed that nothing was impossible and laid 417 miles of track one summer to prove it. He finished the job by 1885.

The railroads, of course, brought not only settlers but a measure of civilization to the West. Even so, during the days of the Union and Central Pacific's construction, exploratory reconnaissances went on. The army, after the Civil War ended, shifted its cavalry out west to protect settlers from Indians and to conduct a "mopping-up" program of topographical surveys. Some civilian ventures went on as well, such

Below: transcontinental railroad lines laid across North America.

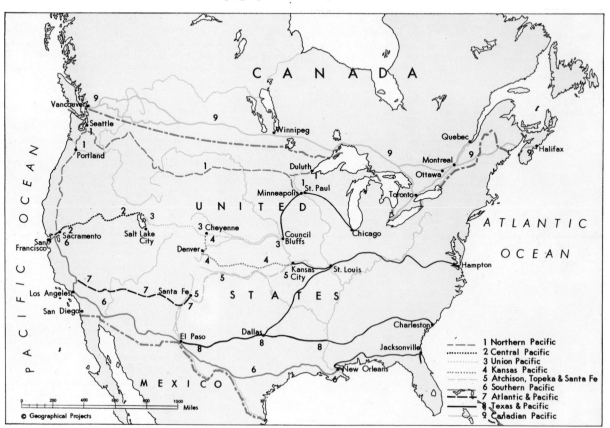

1 Northern Pacific
2 Central Pacific
3 Union Pacific
4 Kansas Pacific
5 Atchison, Topeka & Santa Fe
6 Southern Pacific
7 Atlantic & Pacific
8 Texas & Pacific
9 Canadian Pacific

© Geographical Projects

Making a grass bridge across a swamp.

Col. Stevens

as the one that made a successful tour of the Yellowstone region in 1869. By the early 1870's, Captain W. A. Jones had found the elusive southern entrance to Yellowstone Park (Togwotee Pass, from the Wind River Valley). By that time the region had become a national park, thanks to the good offices of many military and civilian explorers who wished to save it from exploitation.

Clarence King returned to the West in the late 1860's to undertake a full-scale survey of the mountainous region along the 40th parallel in northern Nevada, Utah, Colorado, and southern Wyoming. King needed all his boundless energy to keep the reconnaissance going in the face of a summer heatwave, malaria among his men, and his own temporary collapse after being struck by lightning. His survey was spectacularly successful in its mapping of some of America's most treacherous terrain (including the Black Rock region and the Great Basin). In 1870, having taken a new approach to Mount Shasta, King was the discoverer of the first active glacier to be seen in the United States. It was of major importance in the flurry of geological theorizing about the West's prehistoric development.

King continued his worthwhile discoveries, while, at the same time, a less famous man, Lieutenant George M. Wheeler of the U.S. Army, explored some Nevada and Arizona byways with notable results. He and his men performed a systematic exploration of Death Valley (in heat up to 120°F). They also made a difficult and partial exploration of the Colorado River, because they chose—quixotically—to move

Above: the party that went west with John Stevens, one of the many settlers who traveled to and established themselves in the Midwest. Seen here, the party is piling grass over a swamp to form a bridge.

*up*stream against torrential currents and rapids. Wheeler continued his widespread surveys of isolated and wild areas into the 1870's. By then a civilian explorer, the geologist F. V. Hayden, had entered the field, and his work almost eclipsed that of Wheeler.

Many of Hayden's discoveries were paleontological and not geographical, though no less noteworthy in their own context. For instance, he was the man who first dug up the prehistoric ancestors of the modern horse, although anti-evolutionists dismissed these finds as implied blasphemy (in the same way as Darwinism was dismissed). His work in the Yellowstone area contributed much to the establishment of the national park, as did his other work (in Colorado, for example) to the data-gathering by railroad builders.

And so this pattern of western exploration continued. Men traveled west on hard-living expeditions, and encountered all the difficulties of terrain, weather, wildlife, and Indians then existing. But, as Wheeler said in 1871, "the day of the pathfinder has ... ended." The paths were there, not as ragged Indian trails, but as stagecoach routes and railroad tracks. Towns were built, and ranches, farms, mines, and mills were in operation. But exploration of the West did not stop suddenly. It gradually slowed and mingled with the scientific fact-finding that began in the wild 1840's and went on long after the West had been wholly tamed and won.

Left: a mining tramway in Death Valley near the Nevada border in California. The heat and aridity make Death Valley virtually intolerable during the long hot summer.

Above: Virginia City, Nevada, the
liveliest ghost town in the West.
Oncè the richest city in America,
it remained an important tourist
center after its famous mines—from
which more than $500 million in
gold and silver was extracted from
the Comstock Lode—were exhausted.
The Church of St. Mary's of the Mountains is among the best of the period.

The Disinherited
10

The early explorers of North America must be regarded as the first spearhead of American western expansion. Even the traders and mountain men saw themselves that way, however businesslike or individualistic their primary motives might have been. They believed that the wilderness they roamed rightfully belonged to the United States, and that the aboriginal inhabitants had no more claim to the land than the grizzly bears or coyotes. The Indians were merely part of the landscape and one of the many obstacles that expanding America had to overcome to fulfill its destiny.

This attitude affected every contact between explorers and west-

Above: "The Song of the Talking Wire" by Henry F. Farney. The utter dejection of this Indian, leaning against a telegraph pole as though listening to voices speaking through the wires, outlines the problem, which still exists today, of finding a place for the Indian in modern America.

ern Indians. Of course, these contacts played a relatively minor part in the long, tragic story of America's dealings with the Indians. The actions of explorers had much less impact on Indian relations than full-dress governmental policy, which developed over the decades without any noticeable humanitarian improvements.

Perhaps the process of western expansion must be seen as an un-avoidable culture clash, and one which the Indians could only lose. But it can also be argued that the clash might have been less violent, and that the loss might have been diminished. Instead, American atti-tudes toward the Indians led inexorably to bloodshed and treachery. Whether or not the explorers and Indians met first as friends, or circled each other suspiciously, the end result was the same. The Indian was alienated, and the likelihood of a peaceful settlement between the two groups was made more remote.

From the beginning, white attitudes toward Indians grew out of two primary concepts. First, the Indian was considered an inferior being. He was thought of as not only culturally inferior, but also some-what less than human in his wild savagery, amorality, and godlessness. These views originated from the eastern frontier, where Indian wars had been going on for generations before the Louisiana Purchase. Men who had fought to expand America into Ohio or Kentucky later went into the West with feelings of hate and contempt for all Indians. And even the more thoughtful frontiersmen who admired the Indian peoples upheld the second of these concepts—that the Indians lived on vast areas of valuable land which was rightfully American. Therefore, whether the approach toward the Indian was one of loathing or admiration, the first westerners agreed that the Indian would even-tually have to be pushed aside.

Beforehand, however, the frontiersmen also decided that the Indians could be exploited through trade. Because of this exploitation, the Indian's attitude toward the white man was one of fear and bitterness. Various conflicts on the old frontier also helped to create inter-tribal

Above: an Indian hut on the west coast of America. The primitive lev-el of culture which the early white men found among the tribes led them to the idea that Indians were not only inferior, but also not human.

rivalries, which pitted Indians against Indians on the front lines. The Iroquois learned to hate the French, and the Cherokee, who were fighting for the British, were terrified by the American revolutionaries. The explorer-traders also profited by these traditional Indian enmities, arming some tribes against others. In Canada, the Cree obtained firearms from fur traders and carried out wars against the Blackfoot. In the United States, traders armed the Crow and Flathead tribes against the Blackfoot and sometimes the traders themselves took an active part in the battles that followed. It was not surprising that the Blackfoot struck back against whites as well as Indians, once they too had guns.

At other times, the traders enraged Indians by trying to cut out the middlemen, Indians who had traditionally gathered furs from the deep interior and passed them on to the whites in the Mississippi Valley. The Sioux's attitude toward Lewis and Clark stemmed partly from a fear of being cut out in this way. The Blackfoot, too, opposed the idea of anyone but themselves trading with the mountain tribes.

Below: the tribal Indian areas of North America, with the Eskimos in the far north, showing the Indian migrations and movements in the 1800's.

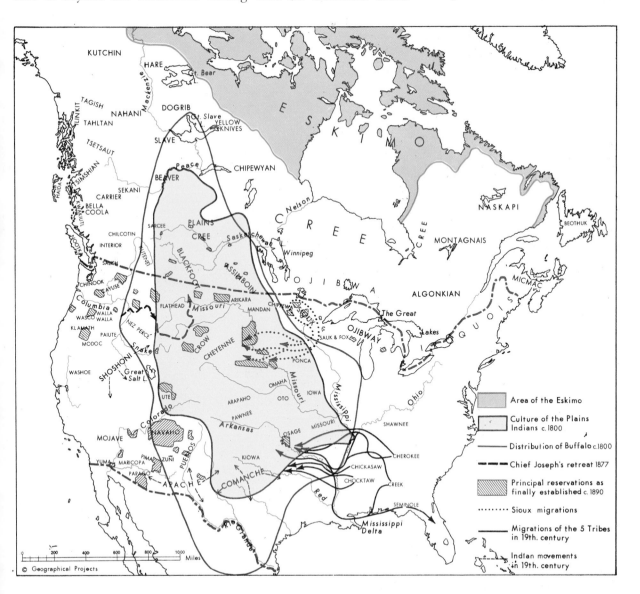

© Geographical Projects

	Area of the Eskimo
	Culture of the Plains Indians c.1800
	Distribution of Buffalo c.1800
	Chief Joseph's retreat 1877
	Principal reservations as finally established c.1890
	Sioux migrations
	Migrations of the 5 Tribes in 19th. century
	Indian movements in 19th. century

Above: however much the early traders may have despised the Indians for their lack of culture, not one of them could deny the great part that the tribesmen played in western trade; either directly by supplying the furs to be traded, or indirectly by acting as guides to the white men.

The trading techniques were also at fault, because many of the traders were ruthless men. For instance, the North West Company thought nothing of cornering a market by extortion, threatening Indians with violence if they dared to trade with rival companies.

Added to these forms of exploitation and alienation were the complications brought by the white man into the West. For instance, the effect of white men's goods on the tribes undermined the traditional Indian skills in a relatively short time. With the availability of iron for axheads and arrowheads, the Indians lost their ability to work stone and flint within a single generation. Therefore, their dependence on the whites, and thus their potential degradation, began almost overnight. Needless to say, the traders were delighted with the situation.

This dependence was further enhanced when the traders offered alcohol to the Indians in exchange for furs. Indian chiefs were well aware of the effect of drunkenness on the tribesmen and loathed the white men because of it. Even worse was the result of diseases which occurred in mild forms in whites but slaughtered the non-immune

Indians by the thousands. In the 1780's a smallpox epidemic killed about one-third of Canada's Plains Indians. Between 1835 and 1860, the United States Plains Indians suffered a similar epidemic, at the time of the first onrush of miners, topographical explorers, and early pioneers. At least half of the Kiowa and Comanche tribes died of a mild cholera in 1849. In the 1870's, another smallpox epidemic swept through the Blackfoot and other tribes, accompanied by rumors that it had been purposefully begun by whites who included infected blankets and clothing among trade goods.

It is not hard to believe that such an early use of biological warfare might have occurred to the white men as an easy and final solution to the Indian problem. Many theorists quite readily suggested extermination of the Indians as a practicable policy to deal with the situation. Certainly the extermination of the buffalo in the late 1800's was explicitly a means of controlling (or wiping out) the Plains Indians.

No one denies that many of the great warrior tribes were given to atrocity (as whites termed it) as normal techniques of war. And no one

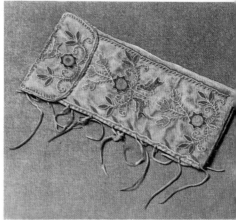

Above: knee-leggings with beadwork, a craft practiced by the Indians, whose traditional handicrafts are only now being fully appreciated.

Left: scalping, one of the Indian "skills" most feared by white men. These sketches demonstrate various gruesome aspects of the art. Pictures show dried scalps being used as decoration on wearing apparel, a horse's harness, and on tepees; the head of a "lucky" victim who has survived the ordeal; and how the scalp was taken.

Below: an attack such as this, by Comanche on a wagon train, became part of the legend of the West. The reasons for such sudden and unprovoked attacks were frequently obscure and those poor unfortunates who were attacked were often the innocent victims of ill-feeling caused by the tribes' previous encounters with hostile white men.

denies that peaceable parties of whites were attacked and massacred for no reason— at least no apparent reason. But it should be remembered that atrocities occurred on both sides. The British anthropologist Peter Farb has suggested that scalping was introduced to the Indians by the whites of the eastern colonies. The colonial authorities actually paid bounties for Indians who were killed, and scalps were taken as proof of the money earned. The practice appeared very early, when New York was still Dutch. By the mid-1700's an Indian scalp taken in Pennsylvania earned the scalper $130.

As for the unwarranted attacks by Indians, it can be understood, if not condoned, that Indians failed to distinguish between dangerous and friendly whites. If a tribe experienced only brutality, contempt, trading swindles, and violence at the hands of the whites, they most likely decided to alter the pattern by violence. Jedediah Smith's men were excusably enraged and embittered by the sudden, unforeseen assault on them by the Mojave (in 1827) who had been friendly the previous year. But Smith's men had no way of knowing about the earlier clash between the Mojave and James Ohio Pattie over a minor trading disagreement, which resulted in an unexpected attack by Pattie on the Indians. Perhaps the Oregonian Indians who jumped Smith's men

The Herald.

EXTRA.

A Massacre

11 Persons Murdered

AT A

Conference at Frog Lake.

Fears Entertained for Battleford.

NAMES OF THE KILLED.

Russian News.

WINNIPEG, April 13.—Telegraphic communication with Battleford was resumed last Thursday, April 8, and news came of a massacre at Frog Lake on April 2 According to it, the Indians invited Acting Sub-Indian Agent Thoma T. Quinn and others to a conference in their camp, and shot them as soon as they entered. Eleven persons were killed.

Father McCombe and some ten settlers are entrenched in the Hudson Bay buildings at Fort Pitt and are surrounded by large numbers of savages. Big Bear's band is amongst them. Great fears are entertained for their fate as well as the fate of the besieged at Battleford who are holding out, but according to the telegram on Thursday were very anxious.

The names of the killed at Frog Lake as far as can be learned are:
Rev. Father Faford.
Rev. Father Terrarch.
Indian Agent Quinn,
Farm Instructor Delaney,
John Goninlock and wife,
J. Williscraft.
Charles German, and three others, names unknown.

Messrs. Delaney, J. K. Simco and two men of the H. B. Co. were taken prisoners

There are 25 police at Fort Pitt. The Stony Indians fired on the police while going to the river for water. In the skirmish which followed two Indians were killed. No whites were injured.
The latest reports say that the situation is unchanged.

Gen. Middleton's force camped yesterday 32 miles from Humboldt, and 10 miles on Salt Plain. Col. Otter has orders to go across the country to Battleford, if the boats are not ready at the mouth of Swift Current to take him down the Saskatchewan.
The York Rangers and the Simcoe Foresters went west to Qu'Appelle and Swift Current last night, and the 9th battalion arrived here. Col. Williams will reach here to-morrow with the Toronto cavalry. The Seventh of London is a day or two behind.

LONDON, April 12 —The Russian force attacked the Afghans at Peijdeh on March 31, and drove them from their position. The Russian accounts say the attack was provoked by the Afghans, but it is believed that the Russians were the aggressors. England is awaiting a satisfactory explanation before declaring war.

Above: a typical report of an Indian massacre which made front-page news in an Extra issued by the Calgary *Herald* on April 13, 1885.

later—or the Comanche who eventually killed Smith—had similar experiences of white violence and treachery festering in their tribe's memory.

But westerners seldom bothered to consider the Indians' provocations. Generally they saw only the horrible results of savage Indian massacres—which sensation-mongering newspapers on the frontier liked to play up, perhaps to justify the United States' policy of pushing Indians out of the way of settlement. But massacres of Indians by white westerners were probably just as great. Sometimes retaliation went to the extreme, such as the infamous Massacre of the Marias that took place in Montana in 1870. Then a detachment of U.S. cavalry, which was pursuing a party of Blackfoot Indians who had stolen some horses, planned an attack on a village of that tribe. The troop killed well over 100 Blackfoot men, women and children.

Of course, these ugly stories do not portray the Indian-Westerner situation in its entirety. In addition to the friendships that grew between certain explorers and western tribes, there were a few early missionaries who went into the northwest to try to pacify the tribes of the region. Men such as the Methodist Jason Lee helped to prepare the Nez Percé and other tribes for the onrush of settlers on the Oregon Trail—and the Nez Percé remained friendly to Americans longer than any other western tribe. It was not until the Nez Percé became exasperated by land-grabbing and encroachments that Chief Joseph reluctantly led his warriors onto the warpath in the late 1870's. This was one of the last of the desperate and futile uprisings that accompanied the entrance of the railroads and the exit of the buffalo.

But good relations between Indians and whites in the United States were always the exception, whereas in Canada they tended to be the rule. Two factors kept them that way—the terrain of Canada and the Hudson's Bay Company policy.

This terrain included the forbidding landscape of the Canadian Shield, which presented an impassable barrier to overland travel above the Great Lakes. Lines of communication for anything larger than a fur trader's canoe simply did not exist between east and west. The Canadian West, then, was the sole preserve of the fur men far longer than in the United States. And while the North West Company may occasionally have provoked Indian wrath, the Hudson's Bay Company laid down an explicit policy of pacification and good relations. Their policy was a paternalistic one through which they hoped to keep

the Indians in a fairly dependent position. Above all, the Hudson's Bay Company had no dreams about a Canadian Manifest Destiny. It actively avoided any general policy of settlement, and the Indians, therefore, had no fears for their land.

The Indians also came to respect British justice, and the British Army, a colonial army which did not have plans or ideas of expansionism. After 1821, when the Hudson's Bay Company ruled the West monopolistically, peace reigned unbroken for decades. Only a trickle of settlers had gone West by the 1860's, and most of them stayed on the fringes of the wilderness. Many missionaries brought the pacifying influence of their religion to the West, and the Northwest Mounted Police maintained law and order and an unswerving tradition of justice. All of this happened long before any massive movement of settlers began to threaten Indian rights and drive them onto reservations. That sort of threat did not materialize until the 1880's, after Canada's transcontinental railroad had thrust into the prairies. By then the familiar missionaries and Mounties had established traditions of peaceful interrelationships that the tribal chiefs found hard to break.

Furthermore, Canada's widespread fur trade had produced a uniquely powerful separate community in its wild west—the *métis* (people of mixed blood). They were predominantly French-speaking, Catholic people who were once wild buffalo-hunting nomads. By the mid-1800's the métis had settled in many areas and held responsible positions in the Hudson's Bay Company. They formed a valuable link—and a buffer—between Indians and white authorities, and were respected and listened to by both sides.

In 1885, though, the métis were led by Louis Riel in Canada's last, and perhaps worst, Indian uprising. There were a number of reasons

Left: the Canadian Shield, a huge, rocky, infertile region curving like a horseshoe around Hudson Bay. Though rich in minerals, it is virtually useless for most agricultural purposes.

Below: the battle of Fish Creek in 1885, between the *métis,* led by Louis Riel, and the Mounties, representing the Canadian government. This was the second uprising by these people of mixed European and Indian blood, who had moved from the Red River Valley to the Saskatchewan River Valley and were afraid that once more they would be dispossessed.

for this revolt. Indians were starving, the buffalo were gone, and governmental policy had grown callous and inept. Nevertheless, many tribes stayed quietly on their reserves during the fighting. Even the Blackfoot remained peaceful—partly through the influence of mounted police and missionaries, and partly because some of the chiefs saw only futility and despair in any attempt to resist the inevitable.

Further warnings about American land-hunger and expansionism existed in abundance east of the Mississippi. On those older frontiers, the spread of American settlement took the invariable form of land grabbing, which included driving out the Indian by force. More usually,

Above: Louis Riel was born in St. Boniface, Manitoba, in 1844. He followed his father as leader of the *métis* and led their protests against the government in 1869 and 1885. After the first uprising failed, Riel was outlawed and fled to the United States for several years. He returned to Canada and was elected to the House of Commons in 1873 and 1874, but was denied his seat. Riel was committed to an insane asylum in 1876 but was freed in 1878. The second rebellion was also a failure and Riel surrendered. He was hanged for treason and his death in 1885 caused an upsurge of religious and racial hatred all over Canada.

though, a quasi-legality was imposed on the acquisitions of Indian land by means of treaties. Treaties were drawn up to conclude frontier hostilities, or they were peaceful agreements by which Indians "ceded" a certain amount of land while retaining portions of their traditional hunting grounds. But, of course, an Indian tribe was more than a little naive in the face of the treaty's "small print." Or, if more shrewd Indian leaders balked at signing, a lesser chief could usually be bribed or coerced into signing away his tribe's lands. If the tribe disowned his authority and tried to reclaim the land, that was considered overt treaty-breaking answerable by force—and a clear American conscience.

Gradually, then, the eastern tribes were pushed farther and farther west as the frontier rolled on. By the late 1700's, the frontier line was being pushed back across the Mississippi. Indians who had given up their ancestral lands in one place were now being shifted off their reserves (set aside by treaty) for smaller, poorer reserves. Some fought, as Tecumseh did in the early 1800's trying to unite the small tribes of the Great Lakes region. But they were crushed, and the broken tribal remnants were more thoroughly dispossessed.

By that time, the removal of Indians had become standard practice. The ruthless idea developed of removing all eastern Indians—what

Above: the life of the Plains Indians was dominated by the buffalo. Their traditional ceremonies honored these animals as the providers of shelter, food, and clothing. Buffalo dances were performed to attract the animals to the hunters, with the men wearing buffalo heads and skins. The arrival of the white men completely changed the way of life of the Indian peoples and their own culture was sharply altered.

there was left of them after the frontier wars—west of the Mississippi. They were to be moved onto unclaimed land in order to join the tribes already wandering there, thereby forming one big Indian Territory. The explorers depended largely on these plans of relocation to deal with the Indians to their own advantage. It was Zebulon Pike who launched this project with his report on the agricultural uselessness of the Great Plains. He stated it bluntly: the pioneers should "limit their extent in the west to the borders of the Missouri and Mississippi, while they leave the prairies incapable of cultivation to the wandering and uncivilized aborigines of the country." In short, the Indians should be pushed into an area that was considered completely useless to the white settlers.

Major Stephen Long's echo of Pike in 1820 speeded up the formulation of this policy. The usual quasi-legal treaties somehow found Indian signatures, and removal of the Indians was rapidly speeded up. The removal remains one of the most brutal and appalling episodes in the history of race relations anywhere. Eastern Plains tribes such as the Osage were pushed off their ancient stamping ground to make way for tribes from Illinois or Kentucky. The Cherokee, who had consciously made themselves a neat little civilized community in Georgia, which included industry, schools, and newspapers, were uprooted by means of deception and force. They were sent west in their "Trail of Tears," a forced march that killed some 4,000 of them. The Great Lakes tribes were pushed westward to meet the same fate. The Seminoles of Florida refused to budge. They vanished into the swamps and fought a bitter guerrilla war made sordid with American atrocity and treachery.

In the end, the eastern frontier was virtually free of large concentrations of Indians. The Plains tribes naturally resented the arrival of "foreign" Indians. And skirmishing made survival even more difficult for the dispossessed forest Indians trying to adapt to prairie life. By the mid-1800's, traders, mountain men, and miners were cluttering the mountains, and the Indians began to feel the pressure of the white presence in the Far West. It was a pincer movement. The Indians saw encroachment and dispossession coming from both sides, and out of bitter desperation, they rose in arms in a last hopeless attempt to turn back the tide.

As tribe after tribe went to war, the railroads and pioneer settlements crept onto the grasslands. The buffalo finally vanished under the

Above right: the lush green, wooded landscape of the Blue Ridge Parkway in North Carolina. About 35,000 Indians lived in North Carolina when the white men first arrived, among them the Cherokees, who lived in the Blue Ridge Mountains. Their reserves were gradually overrun by the white settlers and the tribes were forced to move to smaller, poorer reserves.

Below right: the sort of arid desert terrain to which the Cherokee Indians were moved as the frontiers were pushed farther and farther west.

Below left: Alcatraz Island, once a federal prison in San Francisco Bay, was taken over by Indians after the United States Government found it un-economic as a penal colony. The new possessors have erected signs establishing the island as "Indian land," to which all Indians are welcome.
Below right: San Francisco from Alcatraz Island, the sky-scrapers of the modern city contrasting sharply with the tepee in the foreground.

slaughtering rifles of hunters and soldiers. The army fought with brutal power, inevitably defeating the Indians who were herded onto reservations of poor, worthless land. The Indians even lost some of that in years to come, for Indian policy remained—and to some extent still remains—wide open to bureaucratic mismanagement, and general lack of understanding.

These were the end results of a process that began—in the West—when Lewis and Clark fired their rifles and cannon to impress riverside tribes with American power, or when Pike casually bought the present site of Minneapolis from a local chief. The explorers, government surveyors, scientists, traders, and mountain men perhaps would not have wished such a fate to befall the West's Indian population. But they brought with them the seeds of those inevitable horrors.

The Inheritors
11

By the end of the War of 1812, expansion of the American frontier settlement had taken in Indiana, Ohio, Illinois, and Missouri, and the Mississippi and lower Missouri valleys. The movement then leaped across 2,000 miles to re-establish itself in the empty wilderness of the western mountain states. Expansionism and land hunger may have provoked such a gigantic step, but it actually had been motivated by the fantastic tales of the explorers.

The grand image of the Far West took some time to develop, though, because only a general, rather hazy picture of that area filtered out to the public. This lack of information was partly due to the fact that reports from explorers were given directly to their government sponsors, who did not relay details in their entirety. In addition, the fur traders who followed the forerunners often kept their acquired knowledge to themselves. John Jacob Astor, for instance, did not release the Astorians' reports and maps for many years. As a result it was necessary to rediscover places such as South Pass. For these reasons, the pressure of advancing settlement on the eastern frontiers did not really build up to explosive proportions until a good many years after the War of 1812 was over.

By the time the need to conquer new lands had become irresistible, a sizable bulk of information had been made available. Much of it was highly romanticized, if not downright false. Semifictional accounts of life in the fur trade appeared in quantity. J. O. Pattie's *Personal Narrative,* published in 1831, was one of the most popular, and contained its own set of misrepresentations. None of these publications could be termed adequate guides for would-be settlers of the 1800's. Many of their most notable errors occurred in the geographical data and the maps that accompanied them, and yet such errors often had enough authority behind them to ensure that later cartographers would perpetuate them.

During the 1820's, then, most maps of the West followed William Clark's example of placing the headwaters of the Bighorn and Yellowstone rivers within a stone's throw of the Rio Grande and its Spanish strongholds. Zebulon Pike, too, imposed his idea on several maps that

Left: this picture of golden wheatfields on the Palouse Hills near Colfax, Washington state, shows how settlement and cultivation of the Far West has been established today.

Above: the life of the fur trader was romanticized by many contemporary painters, among them George Caleb Bingham. "The Trappers' Return," which he painted in the mid-1880's, shows trappers returning from a trip, with their canoe laden with skins, watched over by the cat tied securely at the bow of the boat.

somewhere in the central Rockies lay one grand mountain origin of all the Plains rivers. In the same way, certain leading Spanish explorers had earlier believed in the Buenaventura River and had placed it on their maps, and American explorers scoured the West in search of it.

In the 1830's, the professional romanticizers began writing about the wondrous events of the West. The emphasis of such books and newspaper articles was firmly placed on heroism. Publishers saw profits in tales of western adventures, thereby initiating the creation of the western myth. Mountain men and Indian-fighters became immortalized in these literary works.

The trappers and explorers themselves were still publishing their journals and reminiscences. And though these may have glossed over errors and sordid episodes, details of the West were beginning to crystallize and to fire the imaginations of pioneer leaders in the East. For instance, Jedediah Smith wrote a detailed report to the government on the fertile lands of the Columbia Valley, which stated that settlers' wagons could readily be taken through South Pass and northwest into Oregon. This report pointed the way to the creation of the Oregon Trail. At about the same time, the fur trader Joshua Pilcher, head of the Missouri Fur Company, added further stimulus to emigration by

Above: "A new map of North America from the Latest Authorities" by John Cary, Engraver, 1824. This is a fine example of early mapping, showing how the mountains of the Far West were increasingly well-known and accurately shown. Compare the map of 1804 on page 38 to see the progress.

warning about a possible British takeover of the Oregon region, if the United States did not get there first. These reports gained national circulation, as did the later *Narratives* of the clerk Zenas Leonard, who had marched with Joe Walker during the laying out of the California Trail.

By Leonard's time, the reality of a Manifest Destiny had become apparent. His sentiments clearly paralleled those of the majority of his countrymen in their bland assumption that the United States would shortly take over the Far West and civilize it. J. C. Frémont's writings also demonstrated the need and inevitability of such a move. His own dashing image served to accentuate the glamour, excitement, and taste of the West.

But in spite of this new clarity about the West, errors and falsifications still occurred. Landford Hastings, whose distorted geography helped to lead the Donner party into their fearful trap, poured out equally distorted propaganda about the perfections of California. Like other versions of the "guide" to western travel, it contained innumerable inaccuracies. It played down the Indian menace, rarely mentioned the wide deserts or cruel mountain passes, and offered only vague or incomplete information about trails. Richard Henry Dana, in *Two Years Before the Mast*, also glorified the California coast.

At the beginning of the 1850's, one of the most far-reaching misapprehensions about the West still remained firm, that of the Great American Desert. After 1825, according to the historian R. A. Billington, "every literate American believed the region west of the 95th meridian to be a great, unusable desert." Therefore, the explorers were directly responsible for the "leapfrogging" movement of the settlement frontier, from the Mississippi Valley to the mountains.

The leapfrogging process was not readily halted. Although traders, trappers, and early colonists drew groups of settlers to California and Oregon, no nucleus of settlement existed on the central plains. Only millions of buffalo and thousands of wandering Indians were located there. And after mid-century, the American policy of the relocation of Indians to the prairie "wastelands" accentuated the leapfrogging by imposing an even greater barrier to settlement of the plains than climate and topography.

Only when the restless American appetite for unclaimed land and the "taming" of the Plains tribes were satisfactorily fulfilled did settlers begin to encroach on those flat, open grasslands. Previously, they

Above: Joseph Reddeford Walker, a sheriff in Missouri, was one of the great names among mountain men. His finest achievement was his expedition to California in 1833 when he became known as one of the notable pathfinders of the Great West. His party was the first to see and describe the Yosemite Valley. He also acted as a guide to the second overland party to cross the mountains to California.

Right: this page from a geologic
map of the United States shows
the wealth of detail now available
compared to the early maps. This
is, to a large extent, due to the
foundations laid by the explorers.
The different colors indicate
different geologic formations.

not only would not, but decidedly could not make the move. For agricultural techniques of the early 1800's demanded rich loamy soil, a humid atmosphere, and abundant wood. More sophisticated techniques were needed before Americans could turn in any number to "dry farming." Therefore, the cattlemen moved onto the prairies first, realizing that if they could support the gigantic herds of buffalo they could certainly support a few straggly, lean-shanked steers.

The ranchers followed the explorers and early colonists into Texas, Wyoming, and Montana. They left a few ramshackle prairie towns in their wake, and those, plus new farm methods and machinery, opened the doors to full-scale settlement. The settlers learned to build houses and barns of sod, and took advantage of the newly invented barbed wire for their fences. They found out how to use windmills to pump water up from deep-drilled wells and how to plow the shallow soil. Above all, they started to take full advantage of new machinery, and to make greater use of far larger acreages than was ever possible in eastern farming areas.

Meanwhile, of course, the age of exploration had faded away. But the settlers were indebted to the explorers in many ways. The explorers had opened up vast reaches of good land and had determined their extent and main features. Scientists had gathered fine details of terrain and resources which contributed necessary information to

Above: before the Spanish introduced horses into America, the Indians could hunt buffalo only on foot. This they did with moderate success. Sometimes they reasoned that to disguise themselves as wolves gave them an advantage over their huge adversaries. Once they had horses, however, in the 1700's, their prowess as hunters was increased and so began the decimation of the buffalo herds.

Right: settlement of the prairie regions, previously considered infertile and uncultivable, reached its height in the early 1900's. Many of the settlers built their homes from sods, the material most readily and cheaply available. The sods were cut from plowed furrows 12—14 inches wide. A sod-house wall could be anything from 24—30 inches thick. If possible, the roof was made of poles laid across the walls, covered with hay, and the whole thing overlaid with more sods. Sod houses were cool in summer, warm in winter, fire-proof, and would last 20 years or more. They had few windows so were dark inside.

hopeful pioneers. The trails that were laid down by the explorers provided geographical data which helped cartographers to map out accurate routes for the pioneers to come.

Then, too, the early explorers had left in their wake tiny focal points of civilization that later burgeoned into full settlements. From Lewis and Clark's Council Bluffs to the Astorians' trading post on the Pacific and to Sutter's Fort in California, way stations had been scattered across the wilderness. Pioneers going west sometimes stopped at those stations, thereby causing their enlargement. In the northwest, places such as Laramie and Boise dropped the prefix of "Fort" that was used in fur-trading days, and became thriving towns. Santa Fe and Taos swelled into major centers, and Salt Lake City sprang up along an important pioneers' thoroughfare.

And, similarly, old fur-trade posts of the Canadian West rapidly transformed themselves into settlements. The Hudson's Bay Company

moved its Pacific headquarters to Fort Victoria on Vancouver Island, when it saw the inexorable advance of Americans into the Columbia Valley. By the 1850's, it had become western Canada's second true settlement (after Selkirk's colony in what is now Manitoba). Gold seekers in British Columbia, like their earlier counterparts in California, built crude shanty towns to accommodate themselves and their pleasures. When the mining boom died down, some of these towns avoided the slide into ghost-town status and gathered settlers. Trading posts in the interior supported themselves extensively by limited farming of the surroundings. This farming proved the agricultural worth of the land and attracted a trickle of pioneers from eastern frontiers of Canada. The far-reaching explorers of Canada had left behind them the same kind of colonies-in-embryo as had dotted the western United States.

In less than 100 years, therefore, two small clusters of settlements on the eastern seaboard of North America had metamorphosed into

Above: not all settlements prospered, especially those which sprung up quickly around mines. Once the mining boom was over many towns dwindled, and ghost towns like this one at Bodie in California are not an uncommon sight in the West today.

two giant, transcontinental nations. Canada remained a colony until 1867 and did not begin taking proper advantage of her enlarged territories until the present century. The United States began taking advantage from the first day after the Louisiana Purchase. The American destiny, then, *was* manifest—in the sense of the country's ability and willingness to realize in full the potential of its future. And that process of realization began when the first explorers carried out the dream of an American empire as they marched into the West.

Above: looking out across the Golden Gate Bridge, San Francisco—the end of the frontier, the logical conclusion to the story of the western expansion of the United States.

It was hardy gold diggers like these who did much to open up California in the mid-1800's.

Appendix

The opening of the West in the early and middle 1800's was one of the most exciting and adventurous times in United States history. It was also a period in which hardship and suffering were regular occurrences. In order to broaden the view of this remarkable westward movement, the following supplement has been included.

The first section consists of various excerpts from original documents, letters, and articles, which relate in some way to the discovery and settlement of the West. For instance, one of the members of the ill-fated Donner Party described in his journal the horrifying experience of being trapped in the mountains. John Sutter's disappointment in some aspects of finding gold on his land was revealed in the diary he kept at the time. And the methods by which the prospectors actually panned for gold are also described in detail in another extract. The befuddlement of the Wilkinson-Burr conspiracy, "civilizing" the Indians, and the Mormon women's protest for religious rights also contribute to the topics dealt with in this section.

The next part of the supplement includes short biographies of some of the explorers mentioned in the text. Rather than present an entire life history of the men, the biographies deal mainly with the areas that each man was responsible for exploring, the companies or persons for whom he worked, and the dates of his birth and death. To help with these biographies, maps accompany many of those explorers whose journeys are not already mapped elsewhere.

A word glossary has also been included, which follows the biographical section. The glossary should be used as an aid to help the reader define any words or terms that may not already be familiar to him.

For general reference, there is an index to pinpoint specific topics within the text.

Hudson's Bay Company Charter

Pictured here is the royal charter that was drawn up by Charles II of England and granted to the Governor and Company of Hudson's Bay.

"His late Majesty King *Charles* the Second, by Charter under the Great Seal, reciting, That Prince *Rupert,* and divers other Persons therein named, had, at their great Cost, undertaken an Expedition for *Hudson's-Bay,* in the North West Parts of *America,* for the Discovery of a new Passage into the *South-Sea,* and for finding some trade for Furs, and other Commodities; and had there made such Discoveries as encouraged them to proceed further; and had besought his Majesty to incorporate them, and grant them the sole Trade and Commerce of those Parts; and his Majesty being desirous to promote all Endeavours tending to the publick Good, did incorporate them by the Name of, *The Governor and Company of Adventurers* of England *trading into* Hudson's Bay; and did give and grant unto the said Governor and Company, and their Successors, for ever, the

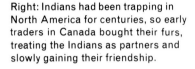

Right: Indians had been trapping in North America for centuries, so early traders in Canada bought their furs, treating the Indians as partners and slowly gaining their friendship.

Left: when the Hudson's Bay Company was formed in 1670 it was given the monopoly of trade round Hudson Bay. Today its agents still go into the wilderness to buy furs from trappers.

Below: trading posts were heavily armed forts, built to protect the traders from the hostile wilderness.

sole Trade and Commerce of those Seas, Rivers, and Lakes, in whatsoever Latitude they should be, that lie within the Entrance of the streights called *Hudson's Streights,* with all the Lands upon the Coasts and Confines thereof, that were not then possessed by or granted to any of his Majesty's Subjects, or possessed by any other Christian State; and the whole and intire Trade and Traffick to and with the Natives and People inhabiting those Parts, and Coasts adjacent."

The Case of the Hudson's Bay Company *(Ordered by the House of Commons to be printed 1749).*

Simon Fraser's Voyage to the Pacific

Simon Fraser and his men, like most explorers of the time, encountered many difficulties in their attempt to reach the Pacific Ocean. In his journal, Fraser relates some of those difficult moments during his trip in 1808.

"**Friday [Thursday], June 23.** Rained this morning. One of the men was sick. We perceived that one way or other our men were getting out of order. They prefered [preferred] walking to going by water in wooden canoes, particularly after their late suffering in the rapids. Therefore I embarked in the bow of a canoe myself and went down several rapids.

"We met some Indians and waited for the arrival of our people, who had gone by land. Walking was difficult, the country being extremely rough and uneven. Passed a carrying place; one of the men fell and broke his canoe almost to pieces. The natives from below came thus far with two canoes to assist us. They were probably sent by our friends who went ahead. In one of the rapids, Mr. Stuart's canoe filled and was nearly lost.

Right: Simon Fraser was an American, born in Vermont, and working for the North West Company in Canada, when he almost reached the Pacific Ocean after traveling overland from the east.

Below left: any expedition traveling along unknown rivers would frequently have to use well-worn Indian portages when the river became too rough or overgrown for their fragile canoes.

Below right: Indians were known to be expert river travelers, but artists and storytellers made their abilities seem heroic, even fanciful.

"Soon after we came to a camp of the natives where we landed for the night. The number of the Indians here may amount to 170. They call themselves Nailgemugh. We met with a hearty welcome from them; they entertained us with singing, dancing, &c.

"The Nailgemugh Nation are better supplied with the necessaries of life than any of those we have hitherto seen. They have robes made of beaver &c. We visited a tomb which was near by the camp. It was built of boards sewed together, and was about four feet square. The top was covered with cedar bark loaded with stones. Near it in a scaffold were suspended two canoes, and a pole from which were suspended [word indecipherable] stripes of leather, several baskets &c.

"The weather was generally very hot in the day time; but at night, being in the neighborhood of eternal snows, it was commonly cold."

The Letters and Journals of Simon Fraser 1806—1808, *ed. by Kaye W. Lamb (The Macmillan Company of Canada Limited: Toronto, 1960) p. 93.*

The Bay Area of San Francisco

During his exploration of California, Jedediah Smith gave this descriptive account, in his journal, of the area around the bay of San Francisco. The entry was dated December 27, 1827.

".... From the S. E. extremity of the bay extends a considerable Salt Marsh from which great quantities of salt are annually collected and the quantity might perhaps be much increased. It belongs to the Mission of St. Jose.

"About one Mile from Santa Clara is the Pueblo which consists of about 100 houses built of the common material. Unburnt Brick. But few of these are any wise respectable in appearance—the remainder are merely huts. Along the east side of the Bay a fine country extends to the Mouth of the Buenaventura River including several fine farms and among the rest that of Santa Ana near the Mouth of the River. On the North Side of the Bay a fine country is spread nearly to the Ocean where there is a chain of Rocky hills nearly on the coast.

".... The farm of Santa Ana extends along the shore of the Bay about three miles and back into the country about the same distance. There is verry little land in cultivation and the amount of stock is small for that country, but the soil is excellent and the situation combining many advantages is at the same time Most Delightful and pleasant."

The Travels of Jedediah Smith, *Maurice S. Sullivan (The Fine Arts Press: Santa Ana, California, 1934) p. 52.*

Above: this advertisement, in the *Missouri Gazette* in February, 1822, encouraged many young men, including 24-year-old Jedediah Smith, to go west in search of fame and fortune.

By 1851, the trails opened by men like Jedediah Smith, and the wealth from the gold strike, helped build San Francisco into a thriving community.

Pattie's Encounter with the Indians

On his way west, James Ohio Pattie had a fierce encounter with the Pipi Indians. The following extract describes in detail that incident of January 1, 1828.

"On this day we once more received a shower of arrows from about fifty Indians of a tribe called Pipi, of whom we were cautioned to beware by the friendly Indians we had last left.... When the Pipi fired upon us, we were floating near the middle of the river.... As soon as our crafts touched the shore, we sprang upon the banks, took fair aim, and showed them the difference between their weapons and ours, by levelling six of them. The remainder fell flat, and began to dodge and skulk on all fours, as though the heavens had been loaded with thunder and mill stones, which were about to rain on them from the clouds.

"We re-loaded our guns, and rowed over to the opposite, and now deserted shore. The fallen lay on the sand beach, some of them not yet dead. We found twenty-three bows and the compliment of arrows, most of them belonging to the fugitives.... They have very large and erect forms, and black skins. Their long black hair floats in tresses down their backs, and to the termination of each tress is fastened a snail shell. In other respects their dress consists of their birth-day suit; in other words, they are perfectly naked."

The Personal Narrative of J. O. Pattie, *ed. by T. Flint (Cincinnati, 1833) pp. 148, 149.*

Thirst and starvation were two very common enemies of any expedition. Above: Pattie described his father and Mr. Slover "...their lips were black... parched mouths wide open..." Below: Pattie, his horse killed for food, said "I loved this horse and he seemed to have an... attachment for me."

The Wilkinson-Burr Conspiracy

Aaron Burr flatly denied any plans of trying to overthrow the United States government in any way. This extract from a letter he wrote to Governor Harrison on November 27, 1806, is a statement to that effect.

"....Considering the various, and extravagant reports which circulate concerning me, it may not be unsatisfactory to you to be informed (and to you there can be no better source of information than myself) that I have no wish or design to attempt a separation of the Union; that I have no connexion with any foreign power or government; I never mediated the introduction of any foreign power or influence, into the United States, or any part of its territories; but on the contrary should repel with indignation, any proposition or measure having that tendency; in fine, that I have no project or view hostile to the interest or tranquillity or Union of the United States, or prejudicial to its government; and I pledge you my honor for the truth of this declaration...."

Aaron Burr compiled a distinguished record during the Revolutionary War before entering the American Senate.

Left: Burr began gathering an army of men along the Ohio River and the question arose: did he mean to overthrow the government or attack Mexico? President Jefferson had him arrested and charged with treason.

Right: on a grassy ledge above the Hudson River across from Manhattan, Aaron Burr, vice-president of the U. S., faced his political rival, Alexander Hamilton. Two shots were heard, Hamilton fell fatally wounded, and Burr fled for his own life.

On June 21, 1807, President Jefferson wrote a letter to Wilkinson, expressing his support of Wilkinson in view of the accusation of treason brought against him.

"....I received, last night, yours of the 16th, and sincerely congratulate you on your safe arrival at Richmond, against the impudent surmises and hopes of the bank of conspirators, who, because they are as yet permitted to walk abroad, and even to be in the character of witnesses until such a measure of evidence shall be collected as will place them securely at the bar of justice, attempt to cover their crimes under noise and insolence. You have indeed had a fiery trial at New Orleans; but it was soon apparent that the clamorous were only the criminal, endeavoring to turn the public attention from themselves and their leader upon any other object....

"Your enemies have filled the public ear with slanders, and your mind with trouble on that account. The establishment of their guilt will let the world see what they ought to think of their clamors; it will dissipate the doubts of those who doubted for want of knowledge, and will place you on higher ground in the public estimate, and public confidence. No one is more sensible than myself of the injustice which has been aimed at you.

"Accept, I pray you, my salutations and assurances of respect and esteem...."

Burr's Conspiracy Exposed; and General Wilkinson Vindicated against the Slanders of His Enemies on that Important Occasion, *James Wilkinson. Introduction 1811. pp. 15–17, 70.*

The Donner Party Catastrophe

Patrick Breen was a member of the ill-fated Donner Party who were trapped in the Sierra Nevada mountains on their way to California. These extracts from Breen's Diary reveal the agony and hardships which the party underwent in the winter of 1846-1847.

"Feb. 23. Froze hard last night. To-day pleasant and thawy; has the appearance of spring, all but the deep snow....

"Feb. 25. To-day Mrs. Murphy says the wolves are about to dig up the dead bodies around her shanty, and the nights are too cold to watch them, but we hear them howl.

"Feb. 26. Hungry times in camp; plenty of hides, but the folks will not eat them; we eat them with tolerably good appetite, thanks to the Almighty God. Mrs. Murphy said here yesterday that she thought she would commence on Milton and eat him. I do not think she has done so yet; it is distressing. The Donners told the California folks four days ago that they would commence on the dead people if they did not succeed that day or the next in finding their cattle, then ten or twelve feet under the snow, and they did not know the spot or near it; they have done it ere this.

"Feb. 28. One solitary Indian passed by yesterday; came from the lake; had a heavy pack on his back; gave me five or six roots resembling onions in shape; tasted some like a sweet potato; full of tough little fibers.

"March 1. Ten men arrived this morning from Bear Valley, with provisions. We are to start in two or three days, and cache our goods here. They say the snow will remain until June."

Above: two of the 32 children, who, with 5 men and 8 women, were the survivors of the 81-strong Donner Party, were Eliza Donner (left), who was 4 years old at the time, and her sister Georgia (right), who was 6.

Below: emigrant families spent their life savings on a wagon, piled it high with all they possessed, and then joined a group heading west. Few knew how to cope with Indians, or even the fundamentals of day-to-day living in the hostile wilderness.

Right: wagon trains had difficulty negotiating the narrow, rock-strewn mountain passes in the summer. But the Donner Party tried to cross the snow-covered Rockies in winter.

In order to make Californians aware of the Donner Party crisis, the *California Star* printed several articles appealing to the public for help. This article was dated January 16, 1847.

"Emigrants on the Mountains

"It is probably not generally known to the people that there is now in the California Mountains, in a most distressing situation, a party of emigrants from the United States, who were prevented from crossing the mountains by an early, heavy fall of snow. The party consists of about sixty persons—men, women, and children. They were almost entirely out of provisions when they reached the foot of the mountains, and but for the timely succor afforded them by Capt. J. A. Sutter, one of the most humane and liberal men in California, they must have all perished in a few days. Capt. Sutter, as soon as he ascertained their situation, sent five mules loaded with provisions to them. A second party was dispatched with provisions for them, but they found the mountains impassable in consequence of the snow. We hope that our citizens will do something for the relief of these unfortunate people."

History of the Donner Party, *C. F. McGlashan (A. L. Bancroft & Company, Printers: San Francisco, 1881) pp. 192, 193.*

There's Gold in Them Thar Hills!

John Sutter, who had organized a thriving establishment in the Sacramento Valley, was a practical man who found the consequences of a gold strike on his property far from desirable. As he confided to his diary, he was far less intrigued with potential gold riches than appalled at the disruption of his normal business.

"....But to the great event! For some obscure reason I saw from the beginning how it would be. The menace of the thing preyed on my mind. Yet I was determined to keep on with my thoughts of empire. The great rush from San Francisco arrived at the Fort in May, 1848. All my friends and acquaintances filled up the houses and the whole Fort. The merchants, doctors, lawyers, sea captains all came up. All was in confusion. My men all deserted me, which is not strange. I could not even shut the gates of my Fort and keep out the rabble without spilling their blood. The immigrants drove their stock into my yards and trampled my grain with impunity....

"The tan-yards were flourishing at this period and the vats were full of leather. All this dried up and rotted—all ruined—and so it was in all the shoe-shops, saddle-shops, boot and blacksmith shops—all were instantly vacated and work was left half completed.... My grist-mill was never finished. Everything was stolen.... My property was all left exposed, at the mercy of the elements and the rabble."

Above: John Sutter, on whose land gold was first found, said "I should have been the richest citizen on the Pacific shore.... Instead of being rich I am ruined... by this sudden discovery."

New Helvetia Diary, *John A. Sutter (The Grabhorn Press: San Francisco, 1939) Introduction pp. xxv, xxvi.*

Gold miners turned quiet townships into extensions of their diggings, making them lawless, crowded places.

Colonel Mason, Governor of California in 1848, wrote a detailed letter to the Secretary of War in which he described the methods of panning gold. This was only one of several observations that Colonel Mason had made during his tours of the gold districts.

"....The day was intensely hot, yet about two hundred men were at work in the full glare of the sun, washing for gold—some with tin pans, some with close-woven Indian baskets—but the greater part had a rude machine, known as the cradle. This is on rockers, six or eight feet long, open at the foot, and its head has a coarse grate, or sieve; the bottom is rounded, with small cleets nailed across. Four men are required to work this machine: one digs the ground in the bank close by the stream, another carries it to the cradle, and empties it on the grate; a third gives a violent rocking motion to the machine, whilst a fourth dashes on water from the stream itself. The sieve keeps the coarse stones from entering the cradle, the current of water washes off the earthy matter, and the gravel is gradually carried out at the foot of the machine, leaving the gold mixed with a heavy fine black sand above the first cleets. The sand and gold mixed together are then drawn off through augur holes into a pan below; are dried in the sun, and afterwards separated by blowing off the sand. A party of four men thus employed at the lower mines averaged a hundred dollars a day."

The Emigrant's Guide to California, *American Topography (Pelham Richardson: London, 1848) Appendix ii.*

Gold mining was either an individual effort or a well-planned joint venture. Above: groups of men, often fathers and sons, joined forces and searched for gold with the help of a cradle. Below: a man working alone would wade into midstream and scoop the river bed into a sieve. The water and fine-grained sand escaped, leaving the gold flashing yellow in the sunshine.

Impressions of Brigham Young

In the late 1800's, a Mormon woman and her family joined their President on a tour of Mormon settlements in the Salt Lake area. Her impressions of her own person-to-person encounter with Mr. Young are vividly described in an extract from her journal.

"I strolled out on the platform afterwards, to find President Young preparing for our journey—as he did every morning afterwards—by a personal inspection of the condition of every wheel, axle, horse and mule, and suit of harness belonging to the party. He was peering like a well-intentioned wizard into every nook and cranny, pointing out a defect here and there with his odd, six-sided staff engraved with the hieroglyphs of many measures; more useful, though less romantic, than a Runic wand. He wore a great surtout [long overcoat], reaching almost to his feet, of dark-green cloth.... lined with fur, a fur collar, cap, and pair of sealskin boots with the undyed fur outward. I was amused at his odd appearance; but as he turned to address me, he removed a hideous pair of green gogles, and his keen, blue-gray eyes met mine with their characteristic look of shrewd and cunning insight. I felt no further inclination to laugh. His photographs, accurate enough in other respects, altogether fail to give the expression of his eyes."

Twelve Mormon Homes Visited in Succession on a Journey Through Utah to Arizona, *(Library of Congress: Philadelphia, 1874) ·p. 5.*

Brigham Young advised Mormons to use handcarts when crossing the American wilderness saying, "...you will find that it will become the favorite method of crossing the plain...."

Below: during pioneer days the Mormon men were allowed to have several wives. This sketch shows part of a Mormon theater reserved for Young's children, the result of his marriages.

We Protest!

In 1886, in Salt Lake City, a mass meeting was held by the Mormon women of Utah at which they violently protested against the federal government's infringement on their religious and voting rights. This is an extract from one of those women's speeches at that meeting.

"Mrs. Marilla M. Daniels

"I, with the women of Utah, do most earnestly protest against Congress legislating to take from us, loyal citizens of the United States, our constitutional rights; rights guaranteed by our forefathers who fought, bled and laid their all upon the altar that they might bequeath to their children the precious boon of liberty; the right to worship God according to the dictates of our own consciences. That right we shall strive to maintain to the best of our ability, without any desire to injure any one, but keep within the pale of peace and justice, allowing all the same privilege that we claim for ourselves....

"We cannot but admire the noble men who had the moral courage, in the face of prejudice and popular feeling, to stand up and speak against such rank injustice.... One might suppose we had no rights that they were bound to respect.... We have been subjected to test oaths, which have deprived many of our citizens of voting or holding office, and now desire to take the franchise from all the women of Utah."

An Appeal for Freedom, Justice and Equal Rights, *Mormon Women's Protest (Desert News Co., Printers: Salt Lake City, 1886) p. 60.*

Left: this family group was typical of the thousands of Mormon families who settled Utah. Notice this man has four wives and seven children.

The American Overland Route

A surveying expedition was organized by the Kansas Pacific Railway Company in the spring of 1867 to find the best route for a southern railway to the Pacific coast through Kansas, Colorado, New Mexico, Arizona, and southern California. William Bell, an Englishman who accompanied the expedition, tells of Indian attacks on the route along the Smoky Hill River, Kansas.

"Never before had hostility to the pale-face raged so fiercely in the hearts of the Indians and never had so large a combination of tribes been formed to stop the advance of the road-makers... every tribe had put on war paint and had mounted their war steeds.

"... The United States Express, carrying... mails, had been organised two years before to run from Denver to the end of the railway advancing along the Smoky Hill River. Stage stations had been built ... twelve to eighteen miles apart, where the stock... was kept, and at which the coaches changed horses. During the winter these coaches ran pretty regularly; but April had scarcely passed before the stages and mail stations became... objects of attack.

"On the night of April 30, Goose Creek Station was attacked, the stock carried off and three mules killed.

"On May the 9th, Monument Station... and Big Timbers Station, were simultaneously attacked, while a third party tried to burn Chalk Bluff Station.

"Two days after, Pond Creek Station... was attacked and fired.

".... The day before they had attacked the stage-coach, and had

Below: for a time the romantic stage-coach and the volatile steam engine traveled side by side. But, as passengers looked for the quickest and most comfortable form of travel, the stagecoach gradually disappeared.

commenced the month of June by scalping and horribly mutilating two frontier men... within a few miles of Fort Wallace. These... took place... while we were at Salina; but in so large and thinly-peopled a country, news of a portion of them only could be expected to reach us.

"As we advanced, every stage or train from the West... told the same tale....

"...We met the overland mail-coach from Denver: the passengers had... to fight their way through and had succeeded in running the gauntlet, with the loss of one soldier killed and one civilian wounded. They had been attacked by twenty-five warriors.... Hoping that the Indians only desired plunder, they threw some of the baggage from the coach and then started their horses off at a gallop, while the half-dozen soldiers on the roof... kept up a brisk fire.

"The coach was riddled with bullets and spattered with blood, so that I was not a little surprised at the remark of the 'lady' passenger ...who... said, 'She had not been much frightened.' I remembered, however, that we were in Kansas...."

Hostilities Commence, *New Tracks in North America, by William A. Bell M.A., M.B., Cantab. Chapman & Hall (London: 1869) pp. 34-36.*

Above: joining the tracks with a golden spike, officials of the Union Pacific Railroad (who started in the east) and the Central Pacific Railroad (from the west), completed the United States' first transcontinental railway. The event took place near Promontory, Utah, in May, 1869.

"Civilizing" the Indians

In 1809, an official was appointed by the President of the United States to formulate and to carry out a plan for civilizing the Indians in the southern part of the country. This is an excerpt from a letter that this gentleman wrote to his friends in Pennsylvania concerning his task.

"I began with the pastoral life, my charge being hunters I recommended attention to raising stock, particularly cattle and hogs.... I next recommended agriculture and raising of fruit trees.... then domestic manufactures; then figures; and lastly, letters. I set examples in all thing myself.... I teach them morality; to be true to themselves; to respect their own rights, and those of their neighbours; and to be useful members of the planet they inhabit.

"On all fit occasions, I inculcate, above all things, an aversion to war, as the greatest curse which can afflict a nation; to be just; to be generous; and, particularly, to protect the stranger and traveler in their land...

"For the first three or four years I experienced a continued rudeness of opposition. In the succeeding three or four, success was slowly progressive...."

Extract of a Letter from a Gentleman appointed to the Superintendence of the Civilization of the Indians, In the southern parts of the United States, *H. B. Politics (Darton and Harvey: London, 1809) p. 41.*

To the Indians the white men were unwanted trespassers. They did not want the "white man's civilization." They had their own which had been successful for centuries. The clash of wills arising from the attempt to transform a complete nation led to many battles, among them Custer's famous Last Stand at Little Bighorn.

Rights of the Indians

The two resolutions reproduced here are only part of those dealing with the rights of the American Indians which were adopted at the Hall of the House of Representatives in Boston, Massachusetts, on January 21, 1830. The whole question of the relationship between the white settlers and the Indians was a subject for growing national concern.

"3. Resolved,

That we consider Indian nations, residing upon lands derived from their ancestors by immemorial occupancy, and never forfeited nor alienated, as having a perfect right, antecedently to any acknowledgement or guaranty on the part of the whites, to retain possession of those lands, and to exclude all other persons; except so far as this perfect right has been modified by compacts, to which the Indians were a party.

"5. Resolved,

That, as the Indian nations were originally independent communities, and exercised full sovereignty over their country, they have a right to retain their ancient form of government, or to alter it according to their pleasure, and to exercise entire sovereignty over their country; except so far as they have consented to a qualified dependence, by treaties with the United States."

Rights of the Indians *(Boston, 1830) pp. 1, 2.*

Above: today many Indians, like this Navaho man, lead much the same lives as their ancestors, managing to blend modern living into their tribal ways. Below: Indians were moved to reservations governed by white men, but many refused to change their customs.

The Explorers

BECKNELL, WILLIAM
1790—1832   Kentucky
1821: He followed a route to the upper waters of the Arkansas River and then went south to Taos and Santa Fe, New Mexico.
1822: Left the Arkansas River near Dodge City and traveled south to the Cimarron River. He followed this river to the South Fork and went over the Divide to the forks of the Canadian River. Traveling across the mountain pass he reached San Miguel, California, establishing the Santa Fe Trail.
1824: Led a trapping expedition to the Green (Colorado) River.

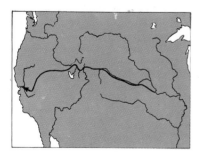

BIDWELL, JOHN
1819—1900   New York
1841: With John Bartleson he formed an emigrant train to go from Missouri to California. They reached Mount Diablo, inland from present-day Oakland.
1846: Went with Frémont to Monterey, California, in the revolt against Mexico. Then returned to Sutter's Fort (Sacramento).

BRIDGER, JAMES
1804—1881   Virginia
1822: Was part of an expedition to trap furs near the source of the Missouri River.
1824: Said to have been the first white man to have visited the Great Salt Lake while on a fur-trapping expedition in Utah.
1843: Established a way-station on the Oregon Trail known as Fort Bridger in the southwest corner of Wyoming.
1849: Acted as guide to Stansbury's expedition to Utah. Returned through Bridger's Pass, south of South Pass, Wyoming.
1859: Accompanied Captain W. F. Raynolds into what is now known as Yellowstone Park.
1861: Guided an expedition in an attempt to find a direct route from Denver, Colorado, to the Great Salt Lake, Utah.
1865: Became involved in an expedition measuring distances on the Bozeman Trail, between Fort Kearny, Nebraska, and Virginia City, Montana.

CLARK, WILLIAM
1770—1838   Virginia
1791-1796: Saw service with the army during the wars with the Indians.
1803: Under the appointment of President Jefferson, he joined with Meriwether Lewis to find a route to the Pacific Ocean. They left St. Louis and went up the Missouri River to the Mandan Villages and on to the foothills of the Rockies. They traveled up a tributary of the Missouri River known as Marias River and then returned to their main waterway, the Missouri. Continuing on up the river to its headwaters they crossed over the watershed to the Columbia River. They traveled down the Columbia to its mouth at modern-day Astoria, California. The expedition then returned down the Snake and Clearwater rivers and across the Bitterroot Mountains to the head of the Jefferson River, Montana. The party then divided. Clark's party went south, crossed the Continental Divide through the Bozeman Pass, down the Yellowstone River to the Three Forks of the Missouri. They were rejoined by Lewis and his party near the mouth of the Yellowstone River and they traveled together down the Missouri and back to St. Louis.
1807: Resigned from the army.
1813: Made governor of the Missouri Territory.
See maps on pages 46-47, 59, 82-83.

CLYMAN, JAMES
1792—1881   Virginia
1823: Joined an expedition, sent out by General William Ashley, traveling up the Missouri River.
1824: Member of the Smith-Fitzpatrick party that traveled to the Green River. They were probably the first white men to go through the South Pass from the east. Clyman separated from the main party on the Sweetwater River, Wyoming, and walked 600 miles east to the Missouri River and Fort Atkinson, Wisconsin.
1826: One of four men to circumnavigate the Great Salt Lake, Utah.
1844: Traveled with an emigrant train to California via Oregon.
1848: Became a guide for emigrant trains traveling from the east to California.

COLTER, JOHN
1775—1813   Virginia
1803: Joined the Lewis and Clark expedition at Louisville, Kentucky.
1806: Left the Lewis and Clark

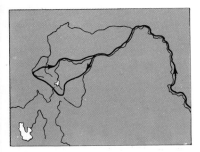

expedition to become a mountain
man, probably wandering in the
Missouri River and Rocky Mountain
areas.
1807: He discovered the area now
known as Yellowstone National Park,
and also several passes through
the Rockies.

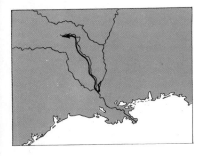

DUNBAR, WILLIAM
1749—1810   Scotland
1798: He was appointed surveyor
general of the District of Natchez
on the southern Mississippi.
He also served as a representative
for the Spanish government defining
and mapping boundaries between the
United States and Spanish
possessions.
1804: Appointed by President
Jefferson to explore the Red River,
from the Mississippi to Texas.
But the party was diverted to
a tributary, the Ouachita River,
by hostile Indians.
1805: Explored the area around
the Red River.

FINLEY, JAMES
1781—1856   North Carolina
1812: Traveled in the woods as
a missionary, and became father
of Wyandott Mission in Upper
Sandusky, Ohio.

FITZPATRICK, THOMAS
1799—1854   Ireland
1823: Joined an expedition as
a trapper going to the upper Missouri.
Also the same year he was second
in command (under Jedediah Smith)
of a small party exploring
Wyoming.
1824: Led the party (again with
Smith) that rediscovered South
Pass in the Bighorn Mountains.
1841: Led the first Pacific-bound
emigrant train with John Bidwell.
Went as far as Fort Hall, Idaho.
1842: Led the White/Hastings
Oregon party to Fort Hall, Idaho.
1843: He acted as guide for
Frémont's second expedition
to the west coast.
1845: Guided Stephen Kearny's
expedition to South Pass.
1846: Continued with Kearny on his
march to California as far as
Socorro, New Mexico. Served two
terms (four years each) as an Indian
agent.

FRASER, SIMON
1776—1862   Vermont
1805: He roamed the Rockies from
Lake Athabasca to the Peace and
Parsnip rivers.
1808: Looking for a route to the
Pacific Ocean he traveled along
the Fraser River as far as the Strait
of Georgia (just south of Vancouver)
where he was turned back by Indians.
See map on pages 34-35.

FRÉMONT, JOHN CHARLES
1813—1890   Georgia
1839-1840: Surveyed the courses of
and land between the Mississippi
and Missouri rivers.
1842: Explored the Kansas River,

Kansas; the North Platte, Nebraska;
and the Sweetwater River, Wyoming,
as far as South Pass. He climbed
Frémont Peak, the highest of the
Wind River Mountains, Wyoming.
1843: Starting from Kansas he
went to Pikes Peak, Pueblo,
Colorado; the Black Mountains,
Wyoming; the Medicine Bow
Mountains, Colorado; the Sweetwater
River; through South Pass to the
Great Salt Lake. He then traveled
north to the Snake River, Idaho, the
Columbia River, Oregon and Fort
Vancouver. Returning around the
Great Basin, Nevada, he went down
the Sacramento Valley and San
Joaquin Valley and across the Sierra
Nevada mountains. He traveled on
up the Spanish Trail to Utah Lake,
across the headwaters of the Platte
River, and back to Pueblo.
1845: Using two different trails,
his divided party crossed the Great
Basin, meeting at Walker Lake at
the foot of the Sierra Nevada.
Dividing again, one party went to
The Tulere Lakes by way of Sutter's
Fort (in present-day Sacramento);
while the other party went via
the Sierra Nevada. Frémont's
group continued north to Klamath
Lake, Oregon, and explored the
Cascade Range.
1848: Leaving Pueblo he went across
the Sangre de Cristo Mountains to
the headwaters of the Rio Grande.
In 1849 he traveled down river to
Taos, New Mexico, and west to
California.
1850: He was elected one of the
first two Senators from California.
1853: Went from Kansas City over
the Wasatch Mountains, Utah,
to Parawan and then turned southwest to the Sierra Nevada.
1856: Nominated for president by
Republican party, but defeated by
Buchanan.
1878: Appointed governor of the
Territory of Arizona.
See maps on pages 82-83, 111

FROBISHER, BENJAMIN

1742(?)—1787.   England
1765: He went into the fur trade.
Later formed a trading company
with his two brothers, Joseph and
Thomas. They did the traveling and
he looked after the Montreal office.

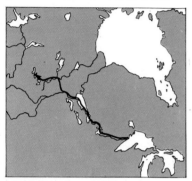

FROBISHER, JOSEPH

1740—1810   England
1769: Attempted to pass beyond
Grand Portage on the U.S./Canadian
border but was turned back by
Indians.
1770: Said to have wintered on
the Red River, but the statement
has been doubted.
1773: Reached Saskatchewan with
his brother, Thomas. Wintered near
the site of Fort Cumberland.
1774: Wintered on the Athabasca
River and nearly died of starvation.

FROBISHER, THOMAS

1744—1788   England
1773: Reached the Saskatchewan
River with his brother, Joseph.
1774: Reached the Athabasca River.
1776: Founded the first trading
post at Ile-a-la-Crosse.

HEARNE, SAMUEL

1745—1792   England
1770: Surveyed the west coast for
the Hudson's Bay Company, traveling inland from Churchill. He
turned north to the Chesterfield
inlet and then went inland to
the Dubawnt Lake.

1771: He went inland to Clinton-
Colden Lake and the mouth of the
Coppermine River. He returned
via the Great Slave Lake.
1774: Established a post at Cum-
berland House on the lower
Saskatchewan River.
See map on pages 34-35.

HENRY, ALEXANDER

1739—1824   New Jersey
After the British conquest of
Canada he was one of the first
traders to reach Michilimackinac
(Mackinac, Michigan).
1764: Traded on Lake Superior.
1776: Reached Cumberland House
and wintered on Beaver Lake.

HUNT, WILSON PRICE

1782(?)—1842   New Jersey
1811: He led an expedition that
left St. Joseph, Missouri, and
traveled west to the Snake River.
The party reached Astoria, Oregon,
(near the site of Fort Clatsop which
had been established by Lewis and
Clark in 1805) the following year.
See maps on pages 82-83, 111.

IVES, JOSEPH C.

1828—1868   New York
1853: As a member of the
Topographical Engineers, he assisted
in a survey of the Pacific Railroad, along the 35th parallel.
1857: He led an expedition along
part of the Colorado River.
See map on pages 118-119.

JUDAH, THEODORE D.

1826—1863   Connecticut
1860: He discovered a railroad
route across the Sierra.

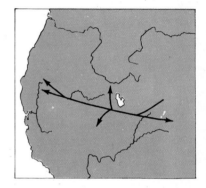

KING, CLARENCE

1842—1901   Rhode Island
1864: Traveled to the Comstock
Lode in Nevada and crossed the
Sierra by foot. Climbed almost
to the peak of Mount Whitney,
then went down the Sacramento
River to San Francisco.
1867: Surveyed the mountainous
region along the 40th parallel,
from eastern Colorado to the
Californian boundary.

LEONARD, ZENAS

1809—1857   Pennsylvania
1831: He joined a party from St.
Louis heading west.
1833: Joined Joseph Walker's
expedition to California at Green
River, Utah.

LEWIS, MERIWETHER

1774—1809   Virginia
1801: Private secretary to President
Jefferson.
1803: Joined with William Clark
in an expedition to find a route
to the Pacific Ocean for Jefferson.
1806: Separated from Clark and the
main party near present-day Missoula
and with a few men crossed the
Divide to the Missouri. They

explored up the Marias River until
they were driven back to the Missouri
by hostile Indians. They met
up with Clark and the rest of the
expedition in Mandan Country.
1807: Became governor of Lousiana
Territory until his death.
See maps on pages 46-47, 59, 82-83.

*For further details of the Lewis and
Clark Expedition see entry under Clark.*

LISA, MANUEL
1772—1820   Louisiana
1807: Headed an expedition up the
Missouri which established trading
posts and forts, including a
trading post at the mouth of the
Bighorn River.
1809: Expedition erected Fort
Lisa on the Missouri River about
10 miles from present-day Omaha.
1811: Led search party up the
Missouri to look for the group
he had left two years earlier.

LONG, STEPHEN
1784—1864   New Hampshire
1817: Examined portages of the
Fox and Wisconsin rivers and explored the upper Mississippi.
1820: Led an expedition to the
Rocky Mountains by traveling along
the Platte River and South Platte
River. He then turned south to
Colorado Springs and headed east

on the Arkansas River and its
tributaries.
1820: Discovered Longs Peak, Colorado.
1823: Explored the sources of the
St. Peter's (Minnesota) River,
and the northern boundary of the
American Great Lakes.
1827-1830: Surveyed railroad routes
for the Baltimore and Ohio Railroad.
See map on pages 82-83.

MACKENZIE, SIR ALEXANDER
1764(?)—1820   Scotland
1789: He left Fort Chipewyan
on Lake Athabasca and traveled
down the Slave River to the Great
Slave Lake. Discovered the
Mackenzie River and followed it
to its mouth.
1792: Left Fort Chipewyan and
followed the Peace and Parsnip
rivers to the Rocky Mountains.
Continued on the Fraser and Bella
Coola rivers, and reached the
Pacific Ocean at Bentinck Arm in
Queen Charlotte Sound. He was the
first white man to travel that ground.
See map on pages 34-35.

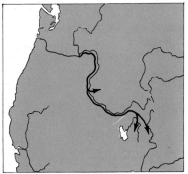

MCKENZIE, DONALD
1783—1851   Scotland
1811: He was a member of Wilson
Hunt's party that traveled to
Fort Astoria.
1816: Led an expedition up the
Columbia River and thoroughly
explored the Snake River, which
opened up trade to southern Idaho.

OGDEN, PETER SKENE
1794—1854   Quebec
1820's: Headed several trapping
expeditions in the valleys of
southern Idaho and eastern Oregon.
1828: One of the first white men
to visit the Great Salt Lake,
Utah. Discovered the Humboldt
River in Nevada.
1829: He led an expedition along
the Colorado River to the Gulf
of California. He became the first
white man to cross the American
West from north to south.
See map on page 111.

PALLISER, CAPTAIN JOHN
1807—1887   Ireland
1847: Led a hunting expedition
in northwestern America.
1857: He commanded an expedition,
sent out by the British government,
to explore British North
America. He traveled between
the 49th parallel in the south
(present U.S./Canadian boundary)
and the 50th parallel in the north
(about 70 miles from present
boundary); the 100th parallel in
the east (through Brandon, Manitoba),
and the 115th parallel in the west
(east of Kimberly, British Columbia.)

PANGMAN, PETER
1744(?)—1819   New England
1767: His name appears in the
Michilimackinac licences as trading
to the Mississippi.

1774: He went fur trading along the Saskatchewan.

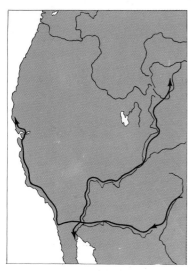

PATTIE, JAMES OHIO
1804—1850   Kentucky
1824: He joined an expedition going to Santa Fe.
1830: Made his way to Cincinnati, Ohio.
1849: Is thought to have joined the gold rush to California.

PIKE, ZEBULON M.
1779—1813   New Jersey
1805: Left St. Louis to find the source of the Mississippi, but went up a tributary, Leech Lake River, to Leech Lake instead.
1806: He led an expedition up the Arkansas River where he discovered Pikes Peak. Searching for the headwaters of the Red River he was taken prisoner by the Spanish. They took him to Santa Fe and Chihuahua, Mexico. He returned to the frontier settlement of Natchitoches on the Red River Louisiana, on his release.
See map on pages 82-83.

PILCHER, JOSHUA
1790—1843   Virginia
1827: He went up the Platte River to its source and penetrated beyond the Rocky Mountains trapping and trading.

POND, PETER
1740—1807   Connecticut
1773: He made two trips from Mackinac, Michigan, to the upper Mississippi and St. Peter's River (now the Minnesota River).
1778: Traveled west via Grand

Portage on the shores of Lake Superior (on the U.S./Canadian border). He opened a rich fur region around Athabasca (north of modern-day Edmonton, Alberta). *See map on pages 34-35.*

PROVOST, ETIENNE
1782—1850   Canada
1823: He traveled from St. Louis to the Green (Colorado) River. Said to have been the first white man to have seen the Great Salt Lake, Utah. It is possible that he discovered the South Pass in the Rockies the same year.
1834: Guided a party to Bayou Salado, present-day South Park, Colorado. That same year he led a second party to Ham's Fork on the Colorado River.

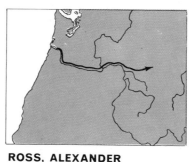

ROSS, ALEXANDER
1783—1856   Scotland
1810: Accompanied an expedition to Oregon and reached a settlement on the Columbia River.
1818: He was a member of an expedition that founded Fort Nez Percé.
1824: Led his own expedition from present-day Eddy, Montana, into Idaho as far as the mouth of the Boise River.

SIMPSON, JAMES HARVEY
1813—1883   New Jersey
1849: Led a party looking for a route between Fort Smith, Arkansas, and Sante Fe, New Mexico. Routed a road from Santa Fe to Navaho Indian country (border of Arizona and New Mexico).
1858: He accompanied an expedition from Salt Lake City, Utah, to the Pacific coast and submitted a report on the new route.
See map on pages 118-119.

SMITH, JEDEDIAH
1798—1831   New York
1822: Went west in answer to Ashley's advertisement for "enterprising young men..."
1823: Traded on the upper Missouri and traveled to the Great Salt

Lake, Utah.
1824: Rediscovered the South Pass, Wyoming, that had been forgotten for over two years.
1826: Left the Great Salt Lake, Utah, and entered California from the Mojave Desert. Traveled to the valley of King's River (near modern-day Fresno) then on to the American River (near modern-day Sacramento) where he crossed the Rockies. He returned to the Great Salt Lake before traveling to winter in the Sacramento Valley.
1828: He reached the mouth of the Klamath River on his way to the Columbia. Traveling north he crossed the Umpqua River, then followed the Willamette River to Fort Vancouver.
1831: He was killed by Indians on the Santa Fe Trail.
See maps on pages 82-83, 111.

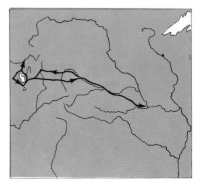

STANSBURY, HOWARD
1806—1863   New York
1835: Surveyed the route of the Mad River, California, and the Lake Erie Railroad. Also the mouths of the Cumberland, Vermilion, and Chagrin rivers.
1836: Surveyed the lower part of the James River, Virginia.
1849: He led a party to explore and survey the Great Salt Lake Region. He left Fort Leavenworth and went to Fort Bridger through South Pass. With Bridger as guide he explored a new route to the lake midway between Bear River and the Echo Canyon Trails.
1850: Again with Bridger as guide he mapped the route of the Union Pacific Railroad that was to follow in his footsteps.

STUART, ROBERT
1785—1848   Scotland
1810: He joined an expedition going to Astoria.
1812: Retraced Wilson Hunt's overland route as far as the Bear

River. Then drifted southeast
and found South Pass, Wyoming.
See maps on pages 82-83, 111.

SUBLETTE, WILLIAM LEWIS
1799(?)—1845   Kentucky
1822: Joined an expedition going
to the Rocky Mountains.
1828: Led his own expedition
to the Rocky Mountains.
Traveled the Oregon Trail
including "Sublette's Cutoff"
and "Sublette's Trace."
1831: Joined the expedition to
Santa Fe, New Mexico, on which
Jedediah Smith was killed.
1832: Traveled again to the Rocky
Mountains.
1834: Chose the site for Fort
William, later Fort Laramie.

THOMSON, DAVID
1770—1857   England
1790: Surveyed for the Hudson's Bay
Company from Cumberland House
to the mouth of the Saskatchewan
River. Then proceeded along the
north shore of Lake Winnipeg, along
the Hayes River to York Factory.
1792: Surveyed the Nelson River.
1797: Severed connections with the
Hudson's Bay Company and joined
the North West Company. Surveyed
from Lake Winnipeg to Lake Superior.
Returned to Lake Winnipeg and crossed
to Lake Manitoba and Lake Winnipeg.
Surveyed down the Assiniboine River.
1798-1799: Reached Cumberland
House in August, wintered on Red Deer
Lake. Reached North Saskatchewan
River and went along the Athabasca
River, passing site of Fort McMurray.
Reached Ile-a-la-Crosse Lake.
1800-1802: Surveyed along the two
branches of the Saskatchewan River.
1807-1811: Setting out from Rocky
Mountain House, surveyed widely in
the Rockies. Built Kootenay House on
the Columbia River. Reached Fort
Astoria in July 1811.
1816: Surveyed the U.S./Canadian
border from the St. Lawrence to the
Lake of the Woods. His great map of
western Canada and other survey work
make him one of the great geographers,
not only of Canada but of the world.
He traveled 50,000 miles and accurately
mapped 1,200,000 square miles of
Canadian and American territory.
See map on pages 34-35.

WALKER, JOSEPH R.
1798—1876   ? Virginia
1820: He was a trapper in New
Mexico until ousted by the Spanish.

Then he moved up to Missouri
and trapped and traded around
Independence.
1832: Was a member of the Benjamin
Bonneville expedition from Fort
Osage to the mountains. He led
the party west from Green River
to the Great Salt Lake, and the
Humboldt and Walker rivers. They
scaled the Sierra (probably the first
white men to do so) and arrived in
Monterey in November, 1833.
1833: Returned across the Sierra
by Walker Pass, through the Great
Basin and Bear River in present-
day Utah.
1843: Led a company of emigrants
to the Pacific coast through Walker
Pass.
1845: Helped guide Frémont's
third expedition to California.
See map on page 111.

WARREN, GOUVERNEUR KEMBLE
1830—1882   New York
1850: Assistant engineer on a
survey of the delta of the Mississippi.
1856: Made maps and surveys of
the Dakota and Nebraska territories.
See map on pages 118-119.

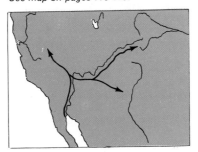

WHEELER, GEORGE M.
1842—1905   Massachusetts
1871: He made 14 trips in the
next 8 years west of the 100th
meridian. He performed systematic
exploration of Death Valley and
partial exploration of the Colorado.

WHITNEY, JOSIAH DWIGHT
1819—1896   Massachusetts
1840: Helped with geologic
survey of New Hampshire.
1847: Surveyed mineral lands
in northern Michigan.
1858: Acted as chemist and
mineralogist for a survey of Iowa.
1860: He was made state
geologist for California.

WOLFSKILL, WILLIAM
1798—1866   Kentucky
1822: Left Franklin, Missouri,
with a Santa Fe expedition.

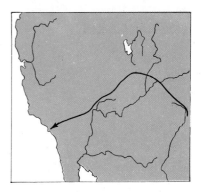

1823: Trapped in the Rio Grande
and was a member of the first party
of white Americans to enter southern
Utah.
1825: Joined Ewing Young trapping
in Gila country, Arizona.
1828: He went with a trading
caravan to New Mexico.
1830: Led a trapping party from
Taos, New Mexico, to California.
Discovered a new route to
California which became known as
the western part of the Spanish Trail.

YOUNG, BRIGHAM
1801—1877   Vermont
1833: Joined the Mormon settlement at Kirtland, Ohio.
1834: Moved with the Mormons to
Far West, Missouri.
1838: When the group was forced
to leave Missouri (people disagreed
with certain of their religious
teachings), he led them to Nauvoo,
Illinois.
1844: He became head of the Mormon
Church after the death of Joseph
Smith, the founder and first leader
of the Mormon religion.
1846-1847: Mormons were expelled
from Illinois and Young led them
to Salt Lake City, Utah.

YOUNG, EWING
(?)—1841   Tennessee
1822: Thought to have been a member
of Becknell's party that opened
the Santa Fe Trail.
1829: He led a party across the
Mojave Desert into California
and trapped along the Joaquin
River.
1831: Organized two expeditions
to California.
1832: Arrived in Los Angeles.
Went on an expedition throughout
California to the Colorado River
at Yuma.
1834: Returned to Los Angeles
and joined an expedition to Fort
Vancouver, Oregon.

Glossary

annexation: The act of adding on, especially new territory.

Apache: Warlike Indians who lived like nomads. Dressed in skins, they wandered in Arizona and New Mexico. Today they are farmers and cattlemen living on reservations in Arizona, New Mexico, and Oklahoma.

Arapaho: These warlike Plains Indians dressed in deerskins. Today they still live in Wyoming and Colorado and during the summer move into tepees and hold ancient ceremonies.

Arikara: In sign language the name of these Plains Indians means "corn eaters." These Indians still live in North Dakota, their original home.

Bella Bella: These Canadian Indians lived in houses of cedar logs. Today they still inhabit British Columbia and Vancouver Island.

Bella Coola: Northwest Indians who originally lived along the Fraser River. This small tribe still lives in British Columbia.

Blackfoot: A group of Plains tribes who lived in Montana, Alberta, and Saskatchewan. They killed the first white trappers on their land so the government paid the Indians guns, ammunition, knives, tools, and glass beads to trap for them. Today this tribe are farmers in Montana and Alberta.

bowie knife: Hunting knife named after Jim Bowie. It is single-edged with a sharp point and a concavely curved back edge and was used as a weapon and an all-purpose tool.

cache: To put something in a hiding place, especially supplies concealed and preserved in the ground.

cantonment: Large camp that is used as quarters for an army or expedition.

Carrier: These northwest Indians lived along the Upper Fraser River.

cartographer: A mapmaker.

caulking: Filling joints and seams of a vessel to make it watertight.

Cherokee: These Eastern Forests Indians lived in Georgia, the Carolinas, and Tennessee. One of the first literate tribes, these farmers had a high cultural level. They now live in the Carolinas and Oklahoma.

Cheyenne: Plains Indians from Minnesota and North Dakota who were once farmers and later buffalo hunters. This warlike tribe, known for their fanatic bravery, today live in Montana and Oklahoma.

Chinook: Lived along the Columbia River in Oregon and Washington. All but the lower classes had sloping foreheads, deformed at birth. Today they live in Washington.

Chipewyan: These Indians, hunters of caribou (deer), lived around the Athabasca Lake and Great Slave Lake in northern Manitoba.

Continental Divide: High ground that separates rivers which are flowing to opposite areas of a continent. The line of summits of the Rocky Mountains forms the Continental or Great Divide.

Comanche: These Plains Indians from Colorado, Kansas, and Texas were the most expert of all Indian horsemen. They could shoot just as straight when hanging under a horse's belly as sitting on his back. Today they live in Oklahoma.

Cree: These Eastern Forests Indians from Manitoba and Saskatchewan were hunters and fishers. Today they are spread right across Canada from Alberta to Quebec.

Crow: Plains Indians from Montana and Wyoming, they were a very wealthy tribe, acting as middlemen in trade between tribes, and becoming scouts for the U.S. Army in the wars with other tribes. They live on reservations in Montana.

Digger Indians: *See Shoshoni.*

dragoon: Someone who served in a military unit as a mounted soldier.

entrepreneur: An individual who manages and assumes the risks of a project, especially a business.

envoy: A person who acts as a representative or diplomatic agent for one group of people to another.

espontoon: a short pike carried by infantry officers in the 1800's.

Flathead: California-Intermountain Indians first seen near Clark Fork. They gathered seeds for most of their food but also hunted buffalo. They still live in Idaho and Montana.

foray: A sudden attack usually made in order to seize goods or valuables.

freebooter: Someone who seeks out goods or valuables by force.

frontier: An area where a developed region meets an undeveloped region.

ghost town: A town that has been deserted by its inhabitants.

homestead: Land acquired from the United States government for living on and cultivating.

interloper: A person who infringes upon the affairs of others.

Iroquois: These Indians lived in upper New York State and formed a federation of tribes. Women nominated members to the tribal council and replaced them if they misbehaved. Today some of the tribes have moved to Oklahoma and Wisconsin but the headquarters of the federation is on Onondaga Reservation, New York.

Kansa: When the government bought this tribe's land in 1873, they named it after them—Kansas. Today these Plains Indians live in Oklahoma.

keelboat: A boat with a keel, allowing it to sail in the wind; roughly built, usually for carrying freight.

Kiowa: Plains Indians who, with the Comanche, raided many ranches in Texas. Today they are farmers living in Oklahoma.

Manifest Destiny: A belief held in the 1800's that it was the mission of the U.S to extend its territory over all the North American continent.

métis: A person of mixed ancestry; in Canada a person of white, usually French, and Indian parentage.

Missouri: Plains Indians who lived along the Missouri River.

Mojave: These Plains Indians, sometimes called Mohave, lived along the Colorado River in the Mojave Desert in southern California.

Mormon: A member of the Church of Jesus Christ of Latter-day Saints, founded in Palmyra, New York in 1830 by Joseph Smith.

Nez Percé: California-Intermountain Indians known for their bravery and almost constant friendship with the white man. Most became Christians. Still live in their home state, Idaho.

Omaha: Plains Indians who lived around present-day Omaha, Nebraska. Now live in Oklahoma and Nebraska.

Osage: Plains Indians who grew corn and hunted buffalo in Arkansas, Missouri, and Oklahoma. When they were moved to Oklahoma, oil was found on their land, making them the richest tribe of Indians in America.

Oto: Semi-sedentary tribe of Plains Indians from along the Missouri. Now in Kansas and Oklahoma.

Pawnee: Plains Indians from Nebraska who never fought against the U.S. One of the few tribes to practice human sacrifice. They sold their white captives as slaves and Pawnee came to mean *slave* to pioneers. Today they live in Oklahoma.

paydirt: A profitable discovery.

pedlars: Canadian fur trappers who sold their furs to companies other than the Hudson's Bay Company.

pemmican: Dried meat beaten into powder and mixed with hot fat and fruits, usually formed into cakes or loaves. It kept indefinitely.

Piegan: A Blackfoot group.

pirogue: A canoe that was formed from the trunk of a tree.

portage: The act of carrying a boat overland around unnavigable water, or from one waterway to another.

Potawatomi: Eastern Forests Indians from Illinois, Michigan, and Wisconsin. They also live in Kansas and Ontario.

Pueblo: Southwest Indians, who were one of the most civilized tribes. These farmers lived in houses often four or five stories high. They still live in Arizona and New Mexico in "pueblos," the Mexican word for "village."

quadrant: An instrument used in navigation to measure altitude.

Seminole: These Eastern Forests Indians from Alabama and Georgia held out against the U.S. government longer than any other tribe. They had two big wars with the white man until peace was finally made in 1934. They now live in Florida and Oklahoma.

Shoshoni: California-Intermountain Indians also called Snake and Digger Indians. They wandered in family groups following the ripening plants. They still live in their home states of Idaho, Nevada, and Wyoming.

Sioux: Plains Indians famous for bravery and fighting ability. The Santee Sioux lived in Minnesota, farming and hunting. The Yankton Sioux farmed and hunted in North and South Dakota. The Teton Sioux hunted buffalo west of the Missouri. Crazy Horse and Sitting Bull were both Teton Sioux. Today the Sioux live in Montana and in North and South Dakota.

squatter: A person who settles on land without the official right or title to do so.

voyageur: The word, which means traveler, was used to describe woodsmen and scouts who were employed by fur-trading companies to move supplies and men through the wilderness. In New France it also meant trappers who operated without a licence.

Walla Walla: Northwest Indians, whose name means "little river," living in Oregon and Washington.

Index

Picture Credits

Listed below are the sources of all the illustrations in this book. To identify the source of a particular illustration, first find the relevant page on the diagram opposite. The number in black in the appropriate position on that page refers to the credit as listed below.

1 Aldus Archives
2 The American Museum in Britain
3 The American Museum in Britain on loan from Department of Archaeology and Ethnography, Birmingham City Museum and Art Gallery/Photo Mike Busselle © Aldus Books
4 The American Museum in Britain/Photo Mike Busselle © Aldus Books
5 Courtesy of The American Museum of Natural History
6 Barnaby's Picture Library
7 Bibliothèque Nationale, Paris
8 Black Star
9 J. Standfield/Black Star
10 British Museum/Photo R.B. Fleming © Aldus Books
11 British Museum/Photo John Freeman © Aldus Books
12 British Museum Newspaper Library/Photo R. B. Fleming © Aldus Books
13 Camera Press
14 Canadian Department of Indian Affairs, Lower Fort Garry
15 Information Service of The Church of Jesus Christ of Latter-day Saints
16 Cincinnati Art Museum
17 City Art Museum of Saint Louis
18 Culver Pictures
19 Western History Department, Denver Public Library
20 The Detroit Institute of Arts
21 Photo R.B. Fleming © Aldus Books
22 Michelle Vignes/Gamma
23 Geographical Projects Limited, London
24 Glenbow-Alberta Institute, Calgary
25 Geoffrey Harrison
26 James Jerome Hill Reference Library
27 Hudson's Bay Company
28 Hudson's Bay Company/ Photo Geographical Projects Ltd
29 Hudson's Bay Company/Photo Michael Holford © Aldus Books
30 The Huntington Library, San Marino
31 Independence National Historical Park Collection, Philadelphia
32 Joslyn Art Museum Collection, Omaha
33 Northern Natural Gas Company Collection, Joslyn Art Museum, Omaha
34 The John Judkyn Memorial, Bath/Photo Mike Busselle © Aldus Books
35 Mansell Collection
36 Metropolitan Toronto Central Library
37 The Minnesota Historical Society
38 Missouri Historical Society, St. Louis
39 Montana Historical Society
40 Josef Muench
41 Museum of Fine Arts, Boston (M. and M. Karolik Collection)
42 National Film Board of Canada
43 National Portrait Gallery, Smithsonian Institution, Washington, D.C.
44 Oregon Historical Society
45 Picturepoint, London
46 Princeton University
47 Provincial Archives of Victoria
48 Public Archives of Canada
49 Public Archives of Canada/Photo John Freeman © Aldus Books
50 Radio Times Hulton Picture Library
51 Photo R. B. Fleming © Aldus Books/Reproduced by permission of the Royal Geographical Society
52 Royal Ontario Museum, Toronto
53 San Jacinto Museum of History Association
54 British Crown Copyright, Science Museum, London
55 Lent to Science Museum, London, by the Royal Meteorological Society
56 George Shepherd, Saskatoon
57 Southern Pacific Company
58 State Historical Society of Wisconsin
59 Stern Archiv
60 The Taft Museum, Cincinnati
61 Life © Time Inc.
62 U.S. Geological Survey
63 United States Information Service, London
64 The Walters Art Gallery
65 Yale University Library

Layout grid of two-page spreads with content numbers:

Spread (pages)	Content
TITLEPAGE	61
4–5	58
6–7	23
8–9	40 / 1
10–11	7 / 35
12–13	23 / 45
14–15	35 / 23
16–17	35 / 25
18–19	35 / 40
20–21	48
22–23	29 / 29
24–25	48 / 11 / 29
26–27	35 27 / 29
28–29	47 / 29
30–31	9 / 14
32–33	45 1 / 4
34–35	23 / 28
36–37	3 1 / 31
38–39	1 / 51 / 17
40–41	5 / 64
42–43	64 / 54 / 54
44–45	64 / 35
46–47	23 / 35
48–49	64 / 6
50–51	3 9 / 35
52–53	11 / 63
54–55	35 / 17
56–57	
58–59	35 / 23
60–61	45 / 31
62–63	31 / 35 33
64–65	23 1 / 64
66–67	40 / 21 / 49
68–69	6
70–71	12
72–73	2 46 / 63 / 44
74–75	11 / 44
76–77	52 / 54
78–79	6 / 64
80–81	3 / 44 / 44
82–83	6 / 23
84–85	19 / 44
86–87	50
88–89	3 3 / 4 / 11
90–91	11 / 34
92–93	11 / 6 / 44
94–95	12
96–97	30 / 40 / 34
98–99	23 / 29
100–101	33 / 33
102–103	30 / 21
104–105	6 / 19 / 19
106–107	64 / 19
108–109	51 / 64
110–111	16 / 23
112–113	53 / 15 / 65 / 35
114–115	23 / 35 / 43
116–117	41
118–119	54 / 55 / 23
120–121	51 / 51
122–123	35 / 4
124–125	57
126–127	6 / 37 / 23
128–129	6 / 63
130–131	6 0
132–133	50 / 23
134–135	6 4 / 3
136–137	50 / 26
138–139	24 / 44
140–141	42 / 56
142–143	24 / 35
144–145	6 / 6
146–147	22 / 59
148–149	63
150–151	20 / 51
152–153	32 / 58
154–155	6 2
156–157	35 / 56
158–159	6
160–161	13 / 35
162–163	35 / 27 5 0
164–165	24 / 36 / 35
166–167	38 / 11 / 50 / 11
168–169	50 / 18 / 18
170–171	10 10 / 35 / 50
172–173	35 / 35 / 35 / 35
174–175	35 / 35 / 35
176–177	35 / 35
178–179	8 / 50 / 37
180–181	23 / 23
182–183	23 / 23
184–185	23 / 23
186–187	
188–189	
190–191	
192	